THE SANTA FE TRAIL
IN AMERICAN HISTORY

William R. Sanford

Enslow Publishers, Inc.

40 Industrial Road   PO Box 38
Box 398   Aldershot
Berkeley Heights, NJ 07922   Hants GU12 6BP
USA   UK
http://www.enslow.com

Library of Congress Cataloging-in-Publication Data

Sanford, William R. (William Reynolds), 1927–
      The Santa Fe Trail in American history / William R. Sanford.
          p.   cm. — (In American history)
      Includes bibliographical references and index.
      Summary: Presents a history of the trail that became an important
commercial route to the southwestern United States during the 1800s.
      ISBN 0-7660-1348-0
      1. Santa Fe National Historic Trail—Juvenile literature. 2. Southwest,
New—History—Juvenile literature. [1. Santa Fe National Historic Trail.
2. Southwest, New—History.]
      I. Title. II. Series.
      F786.S23   2000
      978—dc21   99-037422
                                                                        CIP

Printed in the United States of America

10 9 8 7 6 5 4 3 2 1

To Our Readers: All Internet addresses in this book were active and appropriate
when we went to press. Any comments or suggestions can be sent by e-mail to
Comments@enslow.com or to the address on the back cover.

★ CONTENTS ★

BECKNELL OPENS THE SANTA FE TRAIL

If the Santa Fe Trail had a "father," it was Captain William Becknell. His two journeys to Santa Fe in 1821 and 1822 blazed the path for those who followed.

William Becknell Plans a Trading Expedition

Born in Kentucky in 1790, William Becknell had little education. About 1816, Becknell emigrated to the frontier hamlet of Franklin, Missouri. For a time, Becknell worked there as a salt maker. After searching out salt licks, which are natural deposits of salt in soil, he dug out the salt. Then he sold the salt to other merchants. By 1821, Becknell had become a merchant in Franklin. He stood six feet tall, had red hair, and sported whiskers.

Becknell wanted to see what lay farther west. He invested his small capital in a pack load of trade goods. It included bright calico cloth (brightly colored cloth with figured patterns), iron kettles, needles, and beads. His reputation as a fair trader preceded him. Unlike many peddlers, he did not trade in "firewater" (raw

The Santa Fe Trail stretched from Missouri to New Mexico.

trade whiskey). The American Indians regarded him as trustworthy. They allowed him to move through the Indian Territory without being harmed.

In June 1821, Becknell decided to do something new. He placed an advertisement in the *Missouri Intelligencer*. He wanted to enlist seventy men to join and invest in an expedition that he was organizing. The group would head west to trade for horses and mules. Becknell knew he would have a ready market for these animals among the many new settlers pouring into Missouri.

Becknell to Trade with the Plains Tribes

The advertisement that Becknell placed drew a limited response. By August 4, only five men had applied.

They elected Becknell their captain. The total value of their trade goods was perhaps five hundred dollars. The traders loaded their pack mules carefully. The loads were evenly distributed. If they were not, the mule would try to buck off the packs, or they would lie down and try to rub them off. On September 1, the small group left Franklin. They crossed the Missouri on the Arrow Rock ferry and headed west. Becknell planned to trade with the Comanche. He knew they had many animals stolen from settlers in New Mexico.

Each man carried a muzzle-loading rifle, a powder horn, and a hunting knife. For the most part, the men wore woolen pants and shirts. Their usual buckskin suits would have become uncomfortable when they got wet. Becknell's party threaded its way along the Arkansas River. The plains were black with buffalo. At this point, they had been traveling for two months. Becknell's party struggled up and over Raton Pass (located in what is now southern Colorado). There they spent two days clearing rocks. They were relieved when they again found themselves on open plains. They could travel only eight to fifteen miles per day on their tired horses. On November 13, Becknell chanced upon a group of Mexican soldiers, and braced for trouble. He would not be the first American trader brought to Santa Fe under arrest. As recently as two years before, Davis Merriweather had been imprisoned as a spy.[1]

Soldiers Encourage Becknell to Go to Santa Fe

Becknell was surprised to be greeted "with hospitable disposition and friendly feelings."[2] He and his companions did not speak Spanish. The soldiers did not speak English. Still, the two parties communicated, using a mixture of Spanish, English, Indian, and sign language. Becknell understood their news. Mexico had won its independence. The Spanish trade regulations that banned all imports from the United States were no longer in effect. He would be welcome in Santa Fe. Its people would buy his goods with silver coins. Becknell recognized his good fortune at once. Like all merchants, he was used to taking risks. Becknell took the chance that the Mexican soldiers were telling the truth. Besides, it was already mid-November. The mountain tribes had settled in for the coming winter. Even if Becknell could find them, it might be hard for his party to dispose of their trade goods.

The soldiers provided Becknell with directions. Santa Fe lay less than 150 miles to the southwest. There was an easy route around the southern end of the Sangre de Cristo Mountains. Becknell's party headed for Santa Fe the next day. That afternoon, they reached the village of San Miguel on the Pecos River. The inhabitants welcomed Becknell politely. In San Miguel, Becknell met a Frenchman, who he hired to serve as his interpreter. The next day the group headed south again across mountainous countryside.

Becknell Arrives in Santa Fe

Becknell's party arrived in Santa Fe on November 16, 1821. His arrival coincided with a fiesta that had drawn people into the city from the surrounding area. The arrival of the *Americanos* (the Spanish word for Americans) increased the excitement of the holiday. Becknell recorded in his journal that they "were received with apparent pleasure and joy."[3]

Local young *señoritas* (single Spanish women) offered the weary travelers fruit, sweets, and thin cakes of ground cornmeal called *tortillas*. Soon Becknell's party was surrounded by a noisy crowd. Some people tugged suggestively at the pack ropes. They were ready to trade immediately. Soldiers appeared to help keep order. In no time, Becknell had his mules unloaded and the goods on display. It did not seem to matter how exorbitant the amount the Americans asked for their goods. The people of Santa Fe seemed glad to pay it. There were no goods like these for sale in Santa Fe. They offered to pay with gold and silver, and with turquoise and other semi-precious stones. Soon, each trader had a bulging sack filled with silver *pesos*.

New Mexico's governor, Facundo Melgares, invited Becknell to visit with him. The governor greeted him courteously. The governor hoped that the traders from the United States would keep up contact with his province, his area of jurisdiction. He also would encourage any traders who might wish to emigrate there to set up shop.

Merchants unloaded their goods in the streets of Santa Fe and sold them on the spot.

SOURCE DOCUMENT

"MANIFESTO OF THE PROVISIONAL GOVERNING JUNTA." I READ IN PART:

"THE MEASURES WHICH THE JUNTA HAS PROPOSED IN ORDER TO GUARANTEE AND EXTEND OUR INDEPENDENCE ARE, IN ADDITION TO RALLYING THE PEOPLE, THE ALLIANCE, ASSOCIATION, AND COMMERCE WITH OTHER NATIONS. . . . WITH RESPECT TO FOREIGN NATIONS, WE SHALL MAINTAIN HARMONY WITH ALL, COMMERCIAL RELATIONS, AND WHATEVER ELSE MAY BE APPROPRIATE."[4]

Governor Melgares may have based his welcome to Becknell on an 1821 document that stressed the importance of trade.

Becknell Stays in Santa Fe Only Briefly

Santa Fe was not the splendid city that many Americans had imagined it to be. The town's one-story adobe buildings clustered around a central plaza, which served as the town square. Scraggly cornfields surrounded the town. The town was not large, its population was a little more than five thousand people. In all of New Mexico, there were fewer than forty thousand settlers. Becknell stayed in Santa Fe for only a few weeks.

Winter in the seven-thousand-foot-high city was cold. Nevertheless, Becknell braved the cold because he was anxious to return to Missouri promptly. He did not want to see the New Mexico market overrun by other merchants who would soon follow his example. Thomas James, a St. Louis merchant, had arrived on

December 1 with a shipment of textiles. James tried with little luck to unload his somber-hued fabrics on the color-loving Mexicans. Becknell also wanted to buy new trade goods with his huge profits. One example reveals their size. Miss Fanny Marshall, who lived in Franklin, had invested sixty dollars in the trip. Her brother brought nine hundred dollars back to her.

Becknell now knew that trade with the *Americanos* was welcome. He also knew what goods the New Mexicans wanted. They were fond of calicos, silks and satins, tobacco and whiskey, shoes, rope, black pepper, and hardware of all sorts. He saw they could pay for the goods, not only with money, but also with mules. Becknell left Santa Fe in early December, stopping briefly in San Miguel.

Becknell Returns to Missouri and Plans a Second Try

For the almost eight-hundred-mile return trip, Becknell carried dried meat, coffee, and beans. Becknell left San Miguel on December 13. Only one of his fellow traders accompanied him.[5] The saddlebags of their mules bulged with the profits from the trip. Becknell followed a shorter route along the Cimarron River that avoided the snow-clogged Raton Pass. The frostbitten traders took seven weeks to return to Franklin. They arrived home on January 29, 1822.

One eyewitness, H. H. Harris, described the scene: "Their rawhide packages of silver dollars were dumped on the sidewalk. One of the men cut the thongs and the money spilled out, and clanking on the stone pavement, rolled into the gutter. Everyone was excited."[6]

Becknell's story created great enthusiasm. Another trader was quick to follow Becknell's example. Colonel Benjamin Cooper organized a party of sixteen men. Using packhorses, they headed for Santa Fe on May 6. Each member had two packhorses and about two hundred dollars worth of goods.

Becknell had decided to wait until the spring of 1822 to make his second trip. He spent the next few months organizing. The goods he had ordered arrived in Franklin on a steamboat that had come two hundred miles up the Missouri River from St. Louis.

Becknell's Second Expedition Sets Out

Becknell recruited a party of twenty men. Some would drive the three freight wagons, loaded with goods and pulled by teams of mules. Others would ride on horseback. At last, the prairie grass was high enough to provide feed for the eight mules that pulled each wagon. The wagons carried over five thousand dollars worth of goods. The tightly wedged boxes and bales were carefully stowed so they would not shift on the tortuous trail. The goods were of excellent quality. They included tools and mirrors, trinkets for trade with the American Indians, and clothes and fabrics of many types. Becknell had made sure the textiles were brightly colored because those drew heavy interest.

Becknell did not try to beat the Cooper party to Santa Fe. He knew that his wagons were slower than

Cooper's pack train. His caravan headed west on May 22, 1823.

Almost at once, the Cooper's freight train ran into a band of Osage Indians. Two scouts riding on ahead were robbed, beaten, and taken to an American Indian village. There, Auguste Chouteau, a member of a St. Louis fur trading family, was able to gain their freedom.

Becknell knew that his wagons could not cross the trail over the Raton Pass. He did not want to take the time to build a road there. In western Kansas, Becknell left the route he had traveled earlier. About five miles from present-day Dodge City, his caravan crossed the Arkansas River. Then it headed southwest toward Santa Fe.

Armed outriders on horseback accompanied the wagon trains on the Santa Fe Trail.

Becknell Returns to Santa Fe

Becknell's new route involved traveling across the desert toward the Cimarron River. The traders made sure to fill their canteens. The wagon wheels, each as tall as a man, with an iron rim five inches wide, sank in the sand. Becknell harnessed extra animals. In the mid-June heat, the wagon train stopped by 10:00 A.M. Becknell decided to travel by night. On the treeless plain, he steered by a compass and the stars. For two days, the caravan found no water. Riding ahead, Becknell spotted a buffalo. Its sides were swelled with water. Becknell shot the buffalo, then brought his men with kettles. They slit the buffalo open. Its stomach was filled with water. They drained it off and drank the liquid. Then they followed the buffalo's track to the Cimarron. The worst was over.

Near present-day Las Vegas, New Mexico, Becknell picked up his former trail. When they came within sight of Santa Fe, the men cheered. They did not even pause to clean up. As they rolled into town, they were met with cheers. The *Americanos* had returned. Becknell had successfully brought the first wagon train of goods over the Santa Fe Trail.

★ THE MAGNIFICENT MISSOURI MULE ★

Missouri trader William Becknell ventured west from Franklin, Missouri, in 1821. His announced purpose was to trade for horses and mules. When his party crossed Raton Pass, the riders had to roll rocks aside for their horses to get through. On the return trip, Becknell brought with him a total of four hundred jacks (male donkeys), jennies (female donkeys), and mules (crosses between a male donkey and a female horse). The mules were a New Mexico product. They were descendants of donkeys first imported from Spain in the late 1800s. Mules appear to have the body of a horse. Their heads, ears, and legs more closely resemble donkeys. Mules can have almost any color coat. They range from thirteen to eighteen hands in height.[7] A hand is a unit of measurement equal to 4 inches, or 10.2 centimeters. Some draft mules weighed over a ton. The animals brought home by Becknell were apparently the beginning of the world-renowned Missouri mule.[8] Becknell clearly appreciated the sure-footed mules. When he made the next trip to Santa Fe the following year, he hitched eight of them to each wagon. Mules were costly to buy in Santa Fe. They ranged in price from twenty-five dollars to fifty dollars apiece.

Mules have a number of advantages. They are faster than oxen. Unlike horses, they can live off the prairie grasses. Stronger than horses, mules can pull heavy loads for long distances. They live longer, for twenty to thirty years, and have longer working lives. They rarely become ill or lame. Their hooves are harder than horse hooves, making it unnecessary to shoe them. Mules are very intelligent and quick to learn, and require good training and handling to utilize their intelligence. A well-trained mule can be obliging, kind, tolerant, patient, calm, and sensible. Badly trained mules create problems.

Everyone knows the expression "stubborn as a mule." Mules have a well-earned reputation for being downright cantankerous. One emigrant, John Clark, reported buying several mules before beginning the trip west: "We had to risk our lives in roping them. After being kicked across the pen some half-dozen times and run over as often, we at last succeeded in leading them out. It was laughable." Emigrant Henry Cook voiced the consensus opinion: "What perverse brutes mules are. The beasts! I hate 'em."[9] When mules perceive an order from a human as threatening to their well-being, they are quick to disobey. Mules never take offensive actions against humans. They kick when they are worried that a person may do them harm.

In the freight trains, merchants often fastened one freight wagon behind another.

Mules have three natural gaits, or manner in which they move: the walk, the trot, and the gallop. Others can canter as well, which is slightly slower than galloping. Some breeders produce mules for riding. With training, these mules can refine the trot into a jog and the canter into a lope.

Mules continued to be used as farm animals long after the end of wagon trains. President Harry S. Truman was proud to be the son of a horse and mule trader. He invited a four-mule hitch of Missouri mules to drive in his 1948 Inaugural Parade up Pennsylvania Avenue. The mule was made Missouri's official state animal in 1955. Today Fulton, Missouri, still claims to be the "Mule Capital of the World."

New Mexico has a very long and interesting history.

The Land of the Anasazi

For thousands of years, American Indians lived in the harsh climate of what is now New Mexico. For generations, they lived simply, moving from place to place. They cooked their food using hot stones in closely woven baskets. They learned to plant corn, squash, and beans. They planted seeds, using pointed sticks to dig. About A.D. 700, these people began building simple one-story adobe homes. Four hundred years later, they were erecting multi-story complexes of brick and stone. They formed cities where hundreds, perhaps thousands of people lived. Today we know these people as the Anasazi, from a Navajo word meaning "the ancient ones."

Rainfall was light and undependable in the land of the Anasazi. They developed elaborate water-gathering and irrigation systems to bring water to their fields. The Anasazi had no wheeled vehicles or beasts of burden, yet, they linked their cities with a complex road

2

BACKGROUND OF NEW MEXICO

system. Over these roads, the Anasazi of northwest New Mexico carried two hundred thousand log beams. They brought them to their settlements from forests thirty to fifty miles away. The Anasazi organized their society into clans. Each clan worshiped its nature gods. They performed rites (ceremonies) in circular structures, partly underground, called *kivas*.

This civilization flourished for only a century or two and then collapsed. The Anasazi abandoned their cities. No one is sure why. Archeological evidence tells us there was a roughly two-decade-long drought (1276–99). Other causes may have been warfare, disease, or interruption of trade.

Origin of the Pueblos

Some Anasazi may have moved east to the nearest reliable water source, the Rio Grande. Others probably traveled west, joining the Hohokam along Arizona's Salt and Gila Rivers. A few may have been the ancestors of today's Hopi in western New Mexico. Those who settled on the upper Rio Grande built earth-colored towns. Using clay, stone, and mud, they built box-shaped, flat-roofed dwellings, sometimes four or more stories high. They clustered their homes around a central area. This plaza was not a marketplace or recreation area. It was the site of religious ceremonies and dances.

In the red-cliffed canyons and along the creeks, the Pueblo people prospered. All of the members of a family lived in one room. Most daily activities were

The Spanish of New Mexico lived among the settlements of the Pueblo Indians.

out of doors. The men worked in walled fields growing corn. The women ground and baked the corn. They made pottery, wove cloth, and dressed wild animal skins and fashioned them into clothing. In most pueblos (villages), the women owned the home and everything in it.

The Pueblo continued to divide themselves into clans and societies. They worshiped powerful gods called *kachinas*. They tried to follow the principle of everything in moderation, nothing too much. They attempted to live in harmony with nature. They believed that plants were living beings that would respond if they were spoken to.

The Coming of the Spanish

In 1519, the Pueblo were unaware of events that were taking place far to the south. In Cuba, the Spanish leader Hernando Cortéz heard of a rich empire across the Gulf of Mexico. He organized a small army. Landing at Vera Cruz, Cortéz quickly gained American Indian allies. He led them against the wealthy and powerful Aztec empire. Within two years, Cortéz had conquered the Aztec capital, Tenochitlán. Then transformation of Mexico into New Spain had begun.

In Mexico, the Spanish heard rumors of another golden empire far to the north. In 1539, they sent Father Marcos de Niza to what is now New Mexico. From a distance, he caught a glimpse of the Zuni pueblos. On his return to Mexico City, he identified them. They were, he announced, the fabled golden cities of El Dorado. The following year, Francisco Coronado led an army north into New Mexico. He failed to find either gold or glory for Spain. A priest, Father Jacinto de San Francisco, named the region Nuevo Mexico (New Mexico) in 1561. The Spanish learned more about New Mexico from the expedition of Father Augustín Rodríguez (1581). Eight soldiers and two priests searched unsuccessfully for possible mining sites. The two priests remained behind after the soldiers returned south. They soon lost their lives in an American Indian attack. Two years later, a small expedition led by Antonio de Espejo made the first Spanish contact with the Navajo.

Early Spanish Settlement

The first Spanish settlement of New Mexico took place in 1598. The Spanish viceroy (ruler representing the king) of Mexico sent an expedition led by Juan de Oñate. It included four hundred soldiers and colonists. They brought with them eighty-three wagons of supplies. Their seven thousand heads of stock included cattle, horses, sheep, hogs, and mules. At San Juan, north of present-day Santa Fe, Oñate settled his colony. There he built the first church in New Mexico. From this base, Oñate roamed northeast into Kansas and southwest as far as the mouth of the Colorado.

In 1609, King Philip III of Spain assumed responsibility for the colony. He replaced Oñate as governor with Don Pedro de Peralta. That year, Peralta founded Santa Fe. He made the city the capital of Nuevo Mexico. Peralta ruled from the newly built Palace of the Governors. The structure, which remains standing today, is the oldest public building in continuous use in the United States. Over the next few years, the Spanish established missions among the Pueblos, whom they treated as slaves. The priests used them to work in the fields and on construction projects. A supply train for the missions found its way north from Mexico only once every three years. The Navajo refused to live in the missions. They retreated into the canyons, from which they began raiding Spanish settlements for sheep and horses.

*San Miguel Church in Santa Fe is the oldest church in the
United States.*

Harsh Measures Lead to Revolt

Life in the pueblos was hard. Famine, drought, raiding Apache, and the plague brought death. The colony never produced a profit. The governors tried to squeeze tribute (a tax) from the pueblos. They demanded a yard of cloth or leather and a bushel of corn from each household every year. The priests complained that the Pueblos practiced devil worship. The Pueblos stubbornly refused to give up their traditional ceremonies and dances. To satisfy the priests, in 1680 the governor imprisoned forty-seven medicine men in Santa Fe. He hanged three of them for what he called "sorcery and communication with the devil."

When the Spanish released one man, Popé, from the Tewa Pueblo, he organized a revolt. A cord with a series of knots in it was passed from pueblo to pueblo. Each knot represented a day before the revolt. The uprising was to take place on August 13. All the New Mexico Pueblos were to join in the uprising. Despite the Pueblo precautions, the Spanish learned of the planned revolt. Popé learned that the Spanish had been warned. On August 10, he ordered the attack to occur at once. The Pueblo attacked the missions, and killed the priests. They burned outlying haciendas (ranches) and besieged Santa Fe. The Pueblo succeeded in killing five hundred Spaniards. This was one-fifth of the province's Spanish population. After many days, the Spanish broke through their attackers. They fled hundreds of miles downriver to El Paso.

The Spanish Reconquer New Mexico

The Pueblo victory did not bring with it a return to their former peaceful existence. Popé tried to become a dictator. Civil war against him broke out among the Pueblo. The Spanish made four unsuccessful efforts within eight years to reconquer the province. The plague returned to the Pueblo. Many people abandoned their homes. They moved to join with the Ute in the north and the Zuni and Hopi in the west.

In 1691, the Spanish appointed a new governor, Diego de Vargas, for Nuevo Mexico. The following summer, Vargas led the Spanish forces north up the Rio Grande. His army surrounded Santa Fe. At once, the Spanish cut off the city's water supply. In December, Vargas's men captured the city. Four years of heavy and brutal fighting followed. A second Pueblo uprising failed. Vargas succeeded in subduing the province. Many of the Pueblo fled to live with the Navajo.

When the returning settlers rebuilt their towns, most were in new locations. They opened gold and silver mines in nearby mountains. There was little for them to buy. The Spanish had learned one lesson. They did not demand that the Pueblo totally give up their old ways. Spanish rule was never again as stringent. The Pueblo never again tried to rebel against their rulers.

The Spanish Restrict Trade

In the 1700s, Spanish friars founded chains of missions in Arizona and California. Though there was a trail linking the missions with New Mexico, it was seldom used for trade or travel. Spain followed an economic policy called mercantilism, which meant that colonies and their trade should exist for the benefit of the mother country. There was to be no trade between New Spain and the American colonies along the Atlantic seaboard. Contact was also forbidden with the French, who had linked their Canadian colonies with settlements in Missouri and New Orleans. New Mexico obeyed the law. The province had little contact with the French and Americans.

The Spanish crown had stopped subsidizing the colony. It no longer sent supplies to New Mexico. The settlements were totally dependent on traders in

It took many months for goods to travel in oxcarts from central Mexico to Santa Fe.

Mexico for their manufactured and luxury goods. The Mexicans sent only one mule train a year to Santa Fe. The goods they brought were often second-rate: cheap cloth and poorly made tools. In the latter years of Spanish rule, the Spanish in Santa Fe organized an annual caravan. They journeyed south to the great trade fairs held in Chihuahua and adjoining provinces. They filled great lumbering oxcarts with skins, furs, blankets, and other New Mexico products. They bartered them for clothes, groceries, and items for use in trading with the Pueblo and Navajo.

Mexico Casts off Spanish Rule

In the early nineteenth century, Spain continued to forbid New Mexico from engaging in foreign trade. Trader Robert McKnight of Franklin, Missouri, led a mule pack train and seven men to Santa Fe in 1812. He had heard that the rebel leader Father Hidalgo had overthrown Mexico's Spanish rulers. His information was incorrect. In New Mexico, Governor Manrique confiscated McKnight's goods. He arrested the traders and sent them to prison in Chihuahua. They remained there nine years until Mexico won its independence. The end of Spanish control of New Mexico was approaching. In Europe, Napoleon Bonaparte conquered Spain in 1808. Throughout the Western Hemisphere, colony after colony rose in revolt against Spain. They sought independence from the weakened European masters. On September 16, 1810, a village priest, Father Miguel Hidalgo, began the Mexican

Revolution. Though he was defeated, other leaders followed. Father Morelos, Vicente Guerrero, and Augustín de Iturbide carried on the struggle for independence. The war dragged on for the next decade.

New Mexico took little part in the War of Independence. The ruling group in New Mexico, called *ricos,* remained loyal to Spain. The other classes, the *mestizos* (those of mixed blood), and *péones* (workers and American Indians) knew little and cared less about what was happening far to the south.

Iturbide's army entered Mexico City in August 1821. It was months before word reached New Mexico on December 26. New Mexico was now a Mexican province. It was hungry for trade with the outside world.

★ ZEBULON PIKE ARRIVES IN SANTA FE UNDER GUARD ★

In 1803, President Thomas Jefferson signed the Louisiana Purchase. In it, the United States bought from France much of the land between the Mississippi River and the Rocky Mountains. In 1806, Lieutenant Zebulon Pike received orders to explore the southern portion of the Louisiana Purchase to the sources of the Red and Arkansas rivers. Pike led a twenty-two-soldier team that included a doctor and an interpreter. Pike explored the Front Range of the Rockies. After discovering the peak that now bears his name, Pike became lost in the mountains. His party barely managed to escape with their lives.

Pike led his party southward. In late January 1807, Pike reached the upper Rio Grande, where he built a thirty-six-foot-square fort. On February 7, he sent the party's physician, John Robinson, on to Santa Fe. Three weeks later, a force of Spanish soldiers arrived at Pike's fort. Pike pretended to be surprised that he was on Spanish soil at the Rio Grande. "What, said I, is not this the Red River?"[1] No one was fooled. The Spanish knew in advance that the Americans were sending an expedition into their area. The Spanish soldiers escorted Pike into Santa Fe.

In Santa Fe, curious onlookers studied Pike and his men. Pike wore tattered blue pants and a coat made from a blanket. His scarlet cap was lined with fox skins. Most of his men had long beards and matted hair. They so resembled wild men that someone in the crowd asked whether Americans lived in houses.

The soldiers took Pike to the Palace of the Governors. He told Governor Alencaster that he had not meant to trespass on Spanish soil. Pike lied, and said he had made

In Santa Fe, the Governor's Palace dominated the Plaza.

an honest mistake. The governor asked Pike whether Dr. Robinson had been a member of his party. Pike lied again. He feared the truth would cause Robinson to be convicted as a spy.

Pike and Governor Alencaster met again that night. Alencaster asked to read Pike's papers. After Pike read his orders aloud, the governor shook his hand. He said he was happy to meet a man of honor. Pike thought the danger was past, but Alencaster was no fool. A Spanish officer seized Pike's papers the next day. After he read them, Alencaster was convinced that Pike was indeed a spy.

Alencaster had the power to sentence Pike and his men to death by firing squad. Instead, he gave an order that sent the Americans south into Mexico under military escort. When he heard the order, Pike asked whether he was a prisoner. The governor said no. He did caution Pike not to take any notes of what he would see on the journey, a warning that Pike would ignore. His duty done, Alencaster treated Pike to a fine dinner. Then the governor presented Pike with a farewell gift, one of Alencaster's own shirts.

A troop of cavalry escorted Pike and his men south. Pike reached Chihuahua, Mexico, on April 2. After four weeks in the city, the Spanish escorted Pike's group across northern Mexico and Texas. It was July 1 before Pike reached Natchitoches, Louisiana. From there, he traveled to Washington to make his report.

Pike's report was widely published. It greatly stimulated American interest in New Mexico.

The opening of the Santa Fe Trail was momentous for both the United States and New Mexico.

The United States in 1821

In 1821, the United States was entering a decade of prosperity and expansion. The nation was recovering from the

THE U.S. AND SANTA FE IN 1821

Panic of 1819. The panic had many causes, including wild speculation in Western lands and overexpansion of banks and credit. Also in 1821, President James Monroe began his second term. In the election of 1820, he had won 231 out of 235 electoral votes.

The United States enjoyed new respect overseas. General Andrew Jackson's 1818 campaign against the Seminole Indians in Florida ended successfully for the United States. It led to the Adams Onís Treaty, by which Spain ceded East Florida to the United States. Spain also renounced all claims to West Florida. In 1819, Spain granted Moses Austin colonizing rights in Texas. Following Mexican independence in 1821, his son Stephen Austin traveled to Mexico. The new nation renewed the grant.

The national government was strengthened by a Supreme Court decision. In *McCulloch* v. *Maryland*, the court declared that the federal government possessed implied powers. These were powers needed to carry out those powers listed in the Constitution. In New York, the state abolished the requirement that voters must be property owners. The federal government offered a fifty-dollar bounty for the seizure of every illegally imported slave. The slave trade, abolished in 1807, was declared to be piracy.

Missouri Becomes a State

Settlement in Missouri began along the Mississippi in the 1700s. Following the Louisiana Purchase, settlers flocked into the area. Many moved into the Ozarks of southern Missouri. There they carved farms from the wilderness. They erected log cabins, built furniture, and wove cloth. Missouri became a territory in 1812. Steamboats began to ply the Missouri River in 1819. They traveled as far upstream as Franklin, the future starting point of the Santa Fe Trail. Among their cargoes were flour, whiskey, sugar, and iron castings.

The nation's twenty-two states were evenly divided. There were eleven slave states and eleven free states. In 1821, Missouri became a state. Its admission was based on the Missouri Compromise. The measure had passed by Congress the previous year. It admitted Maine as a free state. Missouri would be a slave state. The law divided the Louisiana Purchase along a line of 36° 30' north latitude. The exception was Missouri,

Much of the goods carried on the trail came up the Missouri River by steamboats such as these.

where slavery was illegal north of the line, but remained legal south of the line. The northern portion was far larger. Southern interests had agreed to the unequal division because they thought the region could never be settled. They called these prairies the Great American Desert.

Americans Look Further West

By 1821, the United States had reached the Rocky Mountains. European nations controlled more than half of the North American continent. Russia controlled Alaska. Canada was a colony of Great Britain. Spain ruled the region between the Rocky Mountains and the Pacific Ocean. Many Americans believed the United States should spread from coast to coast. A newspaper editor, John L. O'Sullivan, gave the concept its name. He wrote, that "the right of our *manifest destiny* [is] to spread over and to possess the whole of the continent which Providence has given us for the development of the great experiment of liberty and federative development of self government entrusted to us."[1]

Believers in Manifest Destiny asserted that America was meant by God to expand its borders. Others simply argued that Americans would use the land more profitably than the American Indians or Europeans could do. These beliefs had taken Americans over the Appalachians into Kentucky and Tennessee. Others had crossed upper New York to Ohio, Indiana, and Illinois. By 1821, Americans were in Florida and on the Gulf Coast. The Mexican provinces of California and New Mexico seemed likely areas for expansion of trade and settlement.

The United States Begins an Industrial Revolution

By 1821, the population of the United States had tripled since independence. The nation's almost ten million residents were swelled in the decade 1821–30 by 143,439 immigrants. Revolutions in manufacturing and transportation were changing the American way of life. The country was becoming more urban. In 1820, Boston and Philadelphia boasted populations of more than fifty thousand. New York had passed the one hundred thousand mark. The country was importing nearly 100 million dollars of foreign goods per year. Newborn American industries relied upon protection from European imports. The government levied a 20 percent tariff on foreign woolens, cotton, and iron goods. Merchants shipped American goods overseas using transatlantic packet ships.

Inventor Eli Whitney contributed to major changes in both the north and south. In 1793, he invented the cotton gin, a machine that allowed one person to clean as much cotton as fifty could by hand. By the early 1800s, cotton was intensely profitable. Planters looked westward for new cotton lands. In 1798, Whitney developed his concept of interchangeable parts. The musket parts his machines produced could be combined and exchanged with all others. Scattered across the country, mills used waterpower to run machines. The first steamboat, Robert Fulton's *Clermont,* began plying American waters in 1807. The age of canals and railroads was waiting in the wings.

New Mexico Battles the Navajo

In 1821, New Mexico's Spanish settlers still waged war with the Navajo, who had migrated into western New Mexico in the early 1500s. The Navajo lived in fixed settlements of extended family groups, or clans They sowed (planted) corn and other vegetables. They raised livestock and wove cloth and fine blankets. Their dependence on livestock and agriculture forced them to remain in their scattered villages. The Navajo were surrounded on three sides by enemies. The Comanche and Ute attacked from the north and east. The Pueblo and Spanish invaded from the east and south.

The Navajo raided the outlying New Mexico ranches to steal sheep and horses. The ranchers responded by sending armed bands to retrieve their livestock. They also captured Navajo women and children to work as slaves. Mexico's independence brought no change in the situation. In 1821, two columns of armed settlers killed dozens of Navajo warriors. They captured many others. In March 1822, the Navajo twice sent leaders to seek peace. All were treacherously murdered.[2] The Navajo gave up their efforts to make peace.

Many New Mexicans Live on *Ranchos*

The Spanish had issued many large land grants in New Mexico. By 1821, thousands of New Mexicans lived on these large estates, called *ranchos*. Their principal income came from sheep raising. The ranchos pastured four million sheep along the Rio Grande.[3] They raised their own food and provided their own protection. The ranchos exported wool and livestock in return for money and finished goods. Workers on the ranchos lived lives of hard toil. Their owners often lived in Santa Fe. Many visited the ranchos rarely. Each rancho was a largely self-sufficient settlement.

The rancho headquarters were fortresslike compounds called *haciendas*. The rectangular structures were made of wood and adobe. Their thick outside

SOURCE DOCUMENT

SIXTEEN NAVAJO CHIEFS CAME. . . . AND REQUESTED THE COMMANDER OF THE FORT TO ALLOW THEM TO PASS ON TO THE GOVERNOR AT SANTA FE, SAYING THEY HAD COME TO MAKE PEACE. THE COMMANDER INVITED THEM INTO THE FORT, SMOKED WITH THEM, AND MADE A SHOW OF FRIENDLINESS. HE HAD PLACED A SPANIARD ON EACH SIDE OF EVERY INDIAN AS THEY SAT AND SMOKED IN A CIRCLE. AT A SIGNAL, EACH INDIAN WAS SEIZED BY HIS SPANISH COMPANIONS AND HELD FAST WHILE OTHERS DISPATCHED THEM BY STABBING EACH ONE IN THE HEART.[4]

Thomas James, an American trader in Santa Fe, describes the murder of the Navajo leaders.

walls had neither windows nor doors. The thick adobe helped keep the structure warm in winter and cool in summer. A hacienda often contained twenty or more rooms. It was built around one or more open areas. Entry was through a large gate that could be closed during attacks. The rooms were dark. They had low ceilings made with woven branches laid between open wooden beams. The family gathered in the largest room. A fireplace provided heat in the cold New Mexico winters. Other rooms included a kitchen, pantry, bedrooms, a granary, cookhouse, and store-rooms for trade goods.

A Traveler Describes Santa Fe

Present-day Santa Fe charms residents and visitors alike. The Santa Fe of 1844 had little such appeal for the outsiders. One visitor wrote:

There was nothing to induce me to entertain the desire to become a resident. . . . The people were nearly all in extreme poverty and there were none who could be classed as wealthy except by comparison. . . . The houses were nearly all old and dilapidated. The streets [were] narrow and filthy, and the people when in best attire not half dressed. . . . On the plaza [was] the government storehouse, or *londiga*. [It was] devoted in ancient times to the storage of corn by the government to sell to the poor and improvident in time of necessity . . . This year [it was] used as a government warehouse to store our goods. From thence south was almost all government buildings.[5]

Some merchants who came to Santa Fe commented negatively about the Plaza and the city.

The Palace of the Governor was part of a larger structure, the *Presidio*. Designed for defense, it formed a four-hundred by eight-hundred-foot rectangle. Several buildings formed parts of its high adobe walls. These included a prison and a chapel. Barracks provided living quarters for Santa Fe's military garrison. Also inside the walls were a small cemetery and a drilling ground.

The People of Santa Fe Fascinate Guests

The traders found the people of Santa Fe exotic, friendly, and attractive. They admired the city's handsome women. Some wore bright red skirts and white blouses. The women did not wear bonnets as American women did. They covered their heads with brightly colored scarves called *rebozos*. Often they pinned flowers in their blue-black hair and painted their lips scarlet. Many smoked cigars in public. Older women often dressed entirely in black. They wore long veils thrown back over their heads. Younger girls often went barefoot all year.

Many of the men wore breeches, tight-fitting leather pants that ended at the knees. A blanket and shirt took the place of coat and vest. A few wealthier men wore large sombreros, hats made of beaver and decorated with gold cords. Their black cloth jackets were decorated with braid. Long silken sashes folded many times circled their waists. Tight pantaloons rose above laced boots. Silver spurs jutted from their boots.

The people of Santa Fe had no newspapers or public schools. Few could read. Travelers marveled that the people of Santa Fe seemed happy and content despite their poverty.

★ FORT OSAGE: ANOTHER STARTING POINT OF THE SANTA FE TRAIL ★

The Louisiana Purchase (1803) was only five years in the past when the United States built Fort Osage. The government built the fort to fulfill a provision of a treaty between the Osage people and the United States. The fort served several purposes. It provided the Osage with a trading post. It helped to enforce the licensing of private traders in the region. It kept out British traders from Canada and Spanish traders from New Spain.

To oversee the building of the fort, President Jefferson chose explorer William Clark. William Boone, youngest son of the famed frontiersman Daniel Boone, was Clark's guide. Clark chose a site on a promontory at a bend of the Missouri River. Clark arrived on September 4, 1808, and he began sketching out the layout of the rectangular fort a day later.

Soldiers dug the eighty-foot-deep well just inside the fort walls. A row of thirty-five cabins formed the western wall of the fort. The cabins housed the families of the fort's soldiers, civilian employees, and artisans. The factory was a three-and-a-half-story trade house. It was one of the few operated by the U.S. government without financial loss. The interpreter's cabin housed the man who translated the French, English, and Osage languages spoken at the fort. The fort boasted four blockhouses. In one or more, guards were on duty twenty-four hours a day. Three of the fort's four officers had apartments in the officers' quarters. The building also housed the fort's day office, where daily business was administered.

The hospital and mess hall were in the same building. A surgeon lived in an apartment there. At one time, the barracks housed eighty-one enlisted men. According to regulations, two men shared a bunk. A soldier's salary was only five dollars per month. The low pay and the absence of women at the fort discouraged enlistment. Punishment, most often flogging, was administered at a disciplinary post near the center of the fort. For a time, Fort Osage was the westernmost U.S. military post. Here many American Indians had their first contact with European Americans.

Up the river by keelboat came traders, trappers, and explorers. They were entering an area whose boundaries were still unclear. The fort soon became a trade center for

Shippers set up headquarters where they brought together animals, men, wagons, and freight.

the Osage, Kansa, and other tribes. It was also a rendezvous for trappers, mountain men, and explorers. Within a few years, the frontier moved farther west. The government closed the fort in 1822. For a few years, the site was an embarkation point for the Santa Fe Trail. Then it was replaced by Independence, Missouri.

In the 1940s, the local residents of nearby Sibley, Missouri, decided to rebuild the fort. They used as many of the original logs and furnishings as they could locate. Today, the fort has been partially restored as a Jackson County park.

Most western trails were routes for people to move into new lands. The Santa Fe Trail was different. From the first, the trail was a trade route. Its users were merchants and their freight caravans.

GATHERING AN EXPEDITION IN INDEPENDENCE, MISSOURI

Newspaper Reports Stir the Imagination

Businessmen in the West were always on the lookout for a new way to make a quick profit. Imagine what they thought when they read this announcement in the *Missouri Intelligencer* of November 10, 1832: "Captain Bent and Company have just returned from Santa Fe with $10,000 in coin, $25,770 in silver bullion, $1,847 in gold bullion, 3,182 pounds of beaver furs, 355 buffalo robes, about 1,300 mules 17 jackasses and 15 jennies. Total value is about $190,000."[1] This was big money at a time when a home could be purchased for a few hundred dollars. For those whose imagination and business sense drew them west, the Santa Fe Trail offered opportunity and romance. It provided travels across plains, deserts, and mountains to a foreign land.

The trail provided them with danger, hardship, and plenty of hard work. Those who plied the trail thought the rewards exceeded the drawbacks.

Franklin, Missouri, Serves as a Beginning Point

The Santa Fe Trail's eastern terminus, or end of the travel route, lay in central Missouri. It lay in what was once the Spanish province of Upper Louisiana. The region became part of the United States in 1803 with the Louisiana Purchase. A decade later, pioneers were laying out towns in central Missouri along the Missouri River. The town of Franklin was laid out in 1816. Three years later there were 120 buildings. Only two were made of brick. A few were built with framed lumber. The rest were log structures. The town's nearly one thousand residents included two hundred slaves. Franklin boasted thirteen shops, four taverns, and two blacksmiths. Its courthouse had cost three hundred dollars.

In one of Franklin's shops, apprentice Kit Carson learned to make saddles. He ran away to become a scout, trapper, trader, and army general. In 1820, ninety-year-old Daniel Boone died in nearby Charette Village. It was from Franklin that trader William Becknell had headed southwest in 1821 to open the route to Santa Fe. In 1828, high water on the Missouri doomed the town, built on the flood plain. A new site, two miles north, became the business center of New Franklin.

Independence Replaces Franklin

After Franklin flooded, traders asked an obvious question: Why walk or drive mules overland when a steamboat could do the job more easily and cheaply? The Missouri River was completely navigable from March until November. The traders looked over a hundred miles westward from Franklin. There they saw Independence, Missouri, a town founded in 1827. The Missouri General Assembly had granted 160 acres to three men. The men surveyed the area and divided it into lots. The lots went on sale for cash or credit. Sixty settlers snapped them up. The Assembly rewarded their success with another eighty acres. The town would serve as the supply point for the farms in the region. It also served the military posts bordering the prairies. The closest was Fort Osage, a dozen miles to the east.

The fledgling town occupied a heavily wooded ridge. Stumps of trees were everywhere, even on the courthouse square. Rough log buildings lined primitive streets that became quagmires after heavy rains. The town was thronged with farmers, trappers, merchants, shopkeepers, and American Indians from several tribes. By 1831, Independence was the Jackson County seat. By 1832, Independence had captured the role of outfitter and point of origin of the Santa Fe Trail. The caravans provided a livelihood for a host of artisans and townspeople. Among them were merchants, blacksmiths, wagon makers, wheelwrights (those who made and repaired wheels, and wheeled vehicles), gunsmiths, saddlers, and harness makers. Neighboring farms sold agricultural products and livestock to the wagon trains.

Steamboats Come Up the Missouri to Independence

By the 1830s, advances in steamboats had cut the month-long voyage from St. Louis to Independence by two-thirds. Travel by boat from St. Louis to Independence eliminated more than 250 miles of poor roads. The town lay near the junction of the Kansas and Missouri Rivers. It was twelve miles from the Indian Territory frontier and two miles south of the Missouri River. Near Independence, the Missouri swung north. Dense forests covered the land east of Independence. Small farms thinly dotted the region. The forests ended abruptly four miles to the west of Independence. Travelers would then find themselves on broad, ocean-like prairies for which there was no end in sight.

Those planning a westward trip usually arrived in Independence about the first of May. Riverboats brought merchandise heading for Santa Fe. They landed four to six miles north of Independence. A blast of the steamboat whistle brought people running. When a steamboat docked, the current pushed it sideways against the bank. Across its gangplanks came the trade goods carried on the backs of black stevedores, whose job it was to load and unload the ships. They sang in chorus as they worked. Shuttle wagons carried heavy loads up the banks. From there they carried their loads down a poor road to waiting freight caravans in Independence. Other goods were stowed overnight under heavy canvas tarps. Amazingly, the goods were not likely to be stolen.

Independence Serves as a Supply and Organization Center

Most of the goods went to the traders who had ordered them. The rest were made available to waiting freighters. Supply houses did the bulk of their year's business in April and May. They handled the food, clothing, boots, shoes, tools, and other necessities that represented a year's luxuries for New Mexico. The empty wagons awaited their loads in the town square. The careful loading of wagons began as soon as their loads were obtained. Most of the goods remained in their original bales and boxes. Only after the goods were loaded would the mules be driven in and placed in harness.

Wagonmasters Take Command

Each wagon train was run by a wagonmaster. His authority over the train was that of a commanding officer. In Independence, he was responsible for loading the freight in the wagons. An improperly packed load could shift, causing the wagon to topple en route. The wagonmaster was the record keeper for the train. He drew up the bills of lading, lists that detailed the goods contained in each wagon. Customs officials at the other end of the trail would check these lists carefully. The lists would serve as the basis on which the goods would be taxed. In addition, the wagonmaster supervised the loading of the goods that would be consumed on the trail. The wagonmaster knew what was needed for each person on the train. The trains loaded fifty pounds of flour and fifty pounds of bacon per person. They also allotted ten pounds of coffee and twenty pounds of sugar per person. Completing the provisions were small amounts of rice, tea, beans, and crackers. The trains relied on hunting buffalo to provide the outfit with fresh meat.

Freight Caravans Employ Bullwhackers and Muleskinners

When the wagons were loaded, it fell to the drovers, the men who drove goods or livestock, to move them out. In pack trains, the drovers were known as muleskinners. The muleskinner was often a Mexican, called an *arriero,* who worked for two dollars to five dollars a month. Each *arriero* supervised eight to ten mules. The mule trains covered twelve to fifteen miles per day. Ox-drawn caravans employed bullwhackers to control their animals. The bullwhackers would whip the oxen if they tried to wander, and these men walked beside their animals in a cloud of dust the eight hundred miles to Santa Fe.

After the trail's early years, when freight wagons replaced pack trains, bullwhackers and drovers received from twenty-five dollars to fifty dollars per month.

Freighters often walked beside their animals for most of the trip along the Santa Fe Trail.

Most of the American muleteers (those who drove mules) and ox drivers came from Missouri. Often, these strong and skillful young men made a trip or two to Santa Fe before settling down back home. Other teamsters, as these team drivers were known, who were seeking adventure, arrived in Independence from throughout the East. Each spring, caravan employees spent their days in Independence waiting for the prairie grass to grow and merchandise to arrive.

Drovers Train Their Animals

Many teamsters spent the time in Independence training their animals. The men usually dressed in a flannel shirt, ragged and stiff with axle grease and pine tar stains. Their trousers were often store-bought jeans, and they wore rough shoes or moccasins. The townspeople of Independence learned to ignore their speech, which was mostly profanity. Legend says a bullwhacker's cursing could strip the bark from an oak tree at up to twenty yards.

To their teams, the drovers were men of few words. These consisted of shouted commands to *Gee!* (Turn right), *Haw!* (Turn left), and *Whoa!* (Stop). The drovers taught their lead, swing, and wheel oxen these words with the help of their whips. Each whip weighed five pounds, and had a sixteen- to twenty-inch handle, and a ten- to sixteen-foot lash. The pop of the whip's buckskin cracker was as sharp as rifle fire.

Large carts carried goods from Santa Fe to other settlements in New Mexico.

Excitement in Independence

For the townspeople, the loading of a Santa Fe caravan was of great interest. They watched from open windows as the wagons received their loads. At starting time, accidents were common. Sometimes the mules refused to move. Sometimes they would bolt in an attempt to flee, dragging the heavy wagon full of merchandise behind them. The loaded vehicle could be overturned by stones or stumps. It sometimes ended up smashing into a log house alongside the trail. It was little wonder that bystanders stood clear as the drivers said their farewells, then snapped their whips.

Westport Landing Replaces Independence

Independence also served as the supply place for the Rocky Mountain fur trade and American Indian traders. In the 1840s, great numbers of those who traveled to the West Coast on the Oregon Trail also outfitted there. The Missouri River constantly washed away the bluffs and docks near Independence. Their remains created a navigation hazard. Steamboat pilots constantly sought out safer landings. By the end of the 1830s, most steamboats were docking a few miles upstream. The site, Westport Landing, would later become part of Kansas City, Missouri. Eventually, Westport Landing replaced Independence, just as Independence had replaced Franklin as the main jumping off point.

SOURCE DOCUMENT

BEFORE ENTERING, [A PACK-TRAIN] GAVE NOTICE BY THE SHOOTING OF GUNS, SO THAT WHEN THEY REACHED OWEN'S AND AULL'S STORE, A GOODLY NUMBER OF PEOPLE WERE THERE TO WELCOME THEM. A GREASY, DIRTY SET OF MEN THEY WERE. WATER, SURELY, WAS A RARE COMMODITY WITH THEM. . . . THEIR ANIMALS WERE LOADED DOWN WITH HEAVY PACKS OF BUFFALO ROBES AND PELTRY [FURS AND SKINS]. OCCASIONALLY THEY HAD A SMALL WAGON, WHICH AFTER LONG USAGE, HAD THE FELLOES [RIMS OF THE WHEELS] AND SPOKES WRAPPED WITH RAWHIDE TO KEEP THE VEHICLE FROM FALLING TO PIECES. SO ACCUSTOMED WERE THEY TO THEIR WORK THAT IT TOOK THEM LITTLE TIME TO UNLOAD THE BURDENS FROM THE BACK OF THE ANIMALS AND STORE THE GOODS IN THE WAREHOUSE. . . . THE ARRIVAL IN INDEPENDENCE WAS ALWAYS A JOYOUS END TO A HAZARDOUS TRIP.[2]

As one eyewitness recalled, the return of a caravan was also an exciting moment.

★ FREIGHT WAGONS ON THE SANTA FE TRAIL ★

For the most part, the Santa Fe Trail was traveled over by freight wagons. They differed from the wagons used to carry settlers west on other trails. On those trails, many immigrants traveled in lighter farm wagons. Others used prairie schooners, half-sized versions of the freight wagons.

By the time the Santa Fe Trail opened, Americans had been making heavy freight wagons for decades. In the East, most freight traveled in Conestoga wagons. These huge freight wagons became one of the mainstays of traffic on the Santa Fe Trail. Made in Pennsylvania, they were shipped down the Ohio and the Mississippi rivers to St. Louis, then up the Missouri River to the unloading points for Independence. The freight wagons were built to haul heavy loads where there was no road. As many as twenty-four oxen drew each wagon. Sometimes drivers attached a second wagon, called a back-action as a trailer. This was called driving *tandem*. The Pennsylvania Dutch first developed the Conestoga wagons. The vehicles were boat-shaped, and had angled ends. Their floors sloped toward the center, so the freight would stay in the wagon rather than jolt out the ends. The wagon builders soaked hardwood boards until they were pliable. Then they bent them into a curve, called a bow and allowed them to dry. Most Conestoga wagons had five bows that formed the tops of the wagons. Over them, the builders stretched high, rounded, white or brown canvas sheets. They doubled and carefully tied down the sheets to make the wagons watertight.

The hardwood wagon box resisted shrinking in the dry air of the plains. The box was two to three feet deep and eleven to twelve feet long. It was beveled to be watertight without caulking. The box sat on two sets of iron-tired hardwood wheels. The rear wheels were larger than the front. They ranged from fifty-four to seventy inches in diameter. The tall wheels held the wagon box well above the center of even the most rutted trail. The wheel's hub, or center, screwed into an iron coiled axle. The wheels had a slight inward slant. On bumpy ground, the slant helped relieve the strain on the spokes caused by the sideways lurch of the bed and the load. The wheel rims were broad, three to five inches wide. Narrower

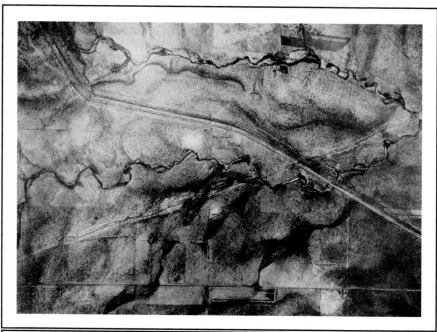

A modern-day aerial photo (top) reveals the Santa Fe Trail ruts still visible in Kansas. On the bottom is a view of trail ruts from the ground level.

wheels cut deeper ruts and were harder to pull. The earlier freight wagons had no braking device.

Ready to roll, the average freight wagon cost $225. Loaded, the four-thousand-pound wagon could carry five thousand pounds of freight.[3] When they left Independence, they presented a bright patriotic picture: white top, red running gear, and blue wagon box.

Conestoga wagons dominated the Santa Fe Trail for thirty years. In time, the New Mexico customs officials began taxing by the wagonload. This caused the traders to turn to larger wagons. First, they used Murphy wagons, made in St. Louis. Then, in 1852, brothers Clem and Henry Studebaker of South Bend, Indiana, began making wagons. Their company grew to be the largest wagon factory in the world.

ACROSS PLAINS, DESERTS, AND MOUNTAINS

Many who traveled the Santa Fe Trail wrote of their experiences. Their writings allow today's reader to relive their journeys.

A Wagon Train Prepares to Move Out

Most days on the trail began when the night herders entered the camp. They sang loudly to awaken the teamsters. The cook began preparing pork and coffee. The bullwhackers began rounding up and yoking the oxen. Experience paid off. Twelve oxen could be ready in little more than a quarter of an hour. When breakfast was over, the wagonmaster shouted "Lave! Lave to!"

> "Catch up! Catch up!" would sound from the captain's camp. It echoed through every division and scattered group. The campground resounds with the gleeful yells of the wagoners [around] me. Each teamster vied with his fellow who shall be soonest ready. It was matter of pride to be the first to cry out, "All's set."
>
> The camp was in an uproar. Teamsters dashed about in pursuit of animals. The unruly brutes called forth shouts from their wrathful drivers. There was,

the clatter of bells, the rattle of yokes and harness, and the jungle of chains. All conspired to produce an uproarious confusion. "All's set!" was directly responded from every quarter. The wagon captain replied at once. "Stretch out!"[1]

Untrained Mules Present a Challenge

The start of a mule-drawn train from Independence could present a far different scene. Early in the morning, the muleskinners drove their animals in from pasture. One by one, they caught the fractious animals with halters. Then they introduced them to the harness. It took fully half a day before the train was ready to begin its long journey.

Thomas Farnham recalled in 1839 what came next, when, early in the journey, the mules were untrained.

It is quite amusing to greenhorns, as those are called who have never been engaged in the trade, to see the

As many as thirty-four oxen could be linked to a team.

mules make their first attempt at practical pulling. . . . The team is straightened and now comes the trial of passive obedience. The chief muleteer gives the shout of march and drives his long spurs into the sides of the animal that bears him; his companion follows his example, but there is no movement. A leer, an unearthly bray [harsh cry], is the only response of these martyrs to human supremacy. Again the team is straightened, again the rowel [point of a spur] is applied, the body-guard on foot raises the shout and all apply the lash at the same movement. The untutored animals kick and leap, rear and plunge, and fall in their harness. After a few trainings, however, of this description, they move off in fine style.[2]

Accidents Were Not Uncommon

Wagon drivers made the most of their last day in Independence. Sometimes they reported to work in

Many freighters preferred mules to oxen to pull their freight wagons.

At Ash Creek we came up with [the wagon train]. The bank, though a little steep, was smooth and there would be no difficulty riding down it. However, we had made up our minds to walk down such places in case of accident, and before we got to it [my husband] hallowed "woe", . . . but as there was no motion made by the driver (the lead animal) to that effect, he repeated it several times and with much vehemence. We had now reached the very verge of the cliff and seeing it a good way and apparently less dangerous than jumping out as we were, he said "go on." The word was scarcely from his lips, ere we were whirled completely over with a perfect crash. One to see the wreck of that carriage, now with the top and sides entirely broken to pieces, could never believe that people had come out of it alive. But strange, wonderful to say, we are entirely unhurt.[3]

This diary entry by Susan Magoffin shows that accidents occurred even to those who were careful.

less than top condition. The four miles between the town and the open prairie were in bad repair. This offered a challenge even to sober drivers. A wagon could end up in a gully. Its load might be strewed down a ravine.

★ A FREIGHT CARAVAN MOVING IN FORMATION ★

A freight caravan on the Santa Fe Trail sometimes resembled a military unit. The wagonmaster took the role of commanding officer. The wagonmaster led each day's journey. Riding at the head of the caravan, he set the pace. Sometimes he rode ahead, scouting for campsites. The wagonmaster selected the spots at which to ford streams. He gave the order each day to "roll on" or "stretch out."

The assistant wagonmaster acted as his aide-de-camp, or second in charge. He brought up the rear. His duties included keeping an eye on the newer drivers and the mess wagon that carried the food and supplies. With him rode the herders who tended the spare mounts and replacement oxen.

Wagonmasters issued general orders to the drivers. They were not to excite their animals by loud "hallooing" or by overusing their whips. They were to be as calm and quiet as possible while yoking up. Ten minutes after leaving a night camp, they were to stop to let the animals rest. They were to rest the animals for two or three hours after covering the first six to eight miles. The drivers were to eat only two meals a day.

Drivers rode horses, and each carried a rifle and a Colt revolver. In mule-drawn trains, the muleskinners rode one of their animals. The paired animals in the front

On the open prairie, freight wagons often adopted a parallel formation while traveling.

were called leaders. Swingers, a younger, less experienced team, occupied a middle position. Wheelers, the mules that were the strongest team, were closest to the wagon. Muleskinners guided their teams with a single rein called a jerk line. In ox-drawn trains, bullwhackers walked on the left side of their animals. They did not use reins. They directed their animals by the accurate use of their whips. Some bullwhackers claimed they could flick a fly off an ear without touching the animal beneath.

Wagons pulled by mules moved at two and a half miles per hour. Oxen moved more slowly at two miles an hour. The difference does not sound like much, yet on the trip from Independence to Santa Fe, a mule train could beat an ox train by a week. Many freighters believed oxen could pull a heavier wagon. This meant a much bigger profit. In 1848, the freight rate from Missouri to Santa Fe was $11.75 per hundred pounds.

The double wing formation was used on open prairie. On narrow trails, this was impossible. The formation was the most preferred one where there was a danger of attack. The two wings could simultaneously swing in a half circle. Wagons parked with their wagon tongues turned inward. They jammed as close to each other as possible, making a solid wall. All of the unhitched livestock could be kept for the night within this corral. There were usually only one or two openings in the circle to enable the riders to enter and leave. If there was little danger of attack, the animals grazed at night outside the corral. Some herders and teamsters were on duty all night as guards.

Nights Are Often Quiet and Beautiful

Writer Matt Field traveled to Santa Fe in the 1830s. He remembered the beauty of nights spent on the trail. He wrote:

> The Arkansas is sweeping by
> Up to the green bank smooth and high.
> The rivers rush and insects hum,
> Are sounds that through the stillness come,
> And the mules, munching their night meal,
> And now and then a quick low squeal,
> As the poor mules approaching stamp
> Disturbs the tenants of the swamp.

For others, night was a time of standing guard. Matt Field recalled:

> Now the moon rides a blue gap, and the shadowy earth is bathed at once in a flood of silver radiance.

What objects are now discernible? There, with their white tops glancing in the moon beam, see the traders' wagons clustering in a group. See the dark forms of the mules and the horses grazing near the wagons; and hear the sounds, the stilly [calm] subdued sounds, so expressive of content, which they make in tearing the green pasturage from the earth, and chewing the juicy mouthful, with their noses lifted in the air. What form sits yonder? Something is crouched in the grass, and muffled in a blanket. Does it move? Hark!

Click! It is the sound produced by the sudden cocking of a rifle, instantly followed by the abrupt demand of "Who's there? Speak?"

"Guard," is the answer. "Your time's up; go in."[4]

Sleeping Arrangements Are Simple

Josiah Gregg remembered sleeping in the open on the Santa Fe Trail:

The camp fires are all lighted outside of the wagons. [There] also, the travelers spread their beds, which consist, for the most part, of buffalo-rugs and blankets. Many content themselves with a single Mackinaw [blanket], but a pair constitutes the most regular pallet [temporary bed]; and he that is provided with a buffalo robe into the bargain is deemed luxuriously supplied. It is most usual to sleep out in the open air, as well to be at hand in case of attack as, indeed, for comfort; for the serene sky of the prairies afford the most agreeable and wholesome canopy. . . . Tents are so rare on these expeditions that in a caravan of two hundred men I have seen not a dozen. In time of rain the traveler resorts to his wagon, which affects a far more secure shelter than a tent. . . . During dry weather, however, even the invalid prefers the open air.[5]

Rivers and Trading Posts Break the Monotony

After a few days on the trail, the trip took on a sameness. River crossings broke up the pattern. They brought a sense of danger and adventure. Only a few trading posts dotted the route. They gave travelers a chance to see new faces and to replenish their supplies.

George Ruxton in 1846 wrote his impressions of a river crossing and the trading post (Bent's Fort) on the northern (Mountain Branch) route of the trail:

> The Arkansas is here a rapid river about a hundred yards in width. The bottom, which is enclosed on each side by high bluffs, is about a quarter of a mile across, and timbered with a heavy growth of cottonwood, some of the trees being of great size. On each side, the vast rolling prairies stretch away for hundreds of miles. . . . Ascending the river the country is wild and broken until it enters the mountains, when the scenery is grand and imposing; but the prairies around it are arid and sterile....The Pueblo is a small fort of adobe with circular bastions at the corners, no part of the wall being more than eight feet high, and around the inside of the yard or corral are built some half a dozen little rooms inhabited by as many Indian traders, coureurs de bois [trappers], and mountain-men. They live entirely upon game, and the greater part of the year without even bread, since but little maize is cultivated.[6]

The Mountains Bring a Change of Scene

The main impression travelers had of the prairies was of their flatness. Yet, unnoticed, the terrain sloped slightly upward. By the time the caravan reached Eastern Colorado, it gradually reached an altitude of almost a mile above sea level. Crossing Raton Pass took the caravan even higher.

Lieutenant W. H. Emory recorded his impressions of the beauty of Raton Pass:

> The height above the sea, as indicated by the barometer, is 7,500 feet. From the summit we had a beautiful view of Pike's Peak, the Wattahyah (Spanish Peaks), and the chain of mountains running south. . . . Several large white masses were discernible, which we at first took for snow, but which, on examination with the telescope, were found to consist of white limestone. . . . For two days our way was strewed with flowers; exhilarated by the ascent, the green foliage of the trees in striking contrast with the deserts we had left behind, they were the most agreeable days of the journey.
>
> The descent is much more rapid than the ascent, and for the first few miles, through a valley of good burned grass and stagnant waters, containing many beautiful flowers. . . . The growth on today's march was pinon in small quantities, scrub oak, scrub pine, a few limita bushes, and, on the Canadian, a few cottonwood trees.[7]

Santa Fe Adapts to Changes

The Santa Fe Trail remained open almost sixty years. By 1880, it was no longer in use as a freight trail. It was a route followed by immigrants and travelers for decades. Santa Fe had changed from a sleepy provincial capital. A railroad spur connected the city to a

Colonel William F. Cody, also known as Buffalo Bill, commented on the Santa Fe Trail.

transcontinental railroad. That same year, a gas company brought light and heat to the city.

William F. Cody, better known as Buffalo Bill, writing in 1897, expressed his feelings about the passing of the Santa Fe Trail this way:

> When the famous highway was established across the great plains as a line of communication . . . , the only method of travel was the slow freight caravan drawn by patient oxen, or the lumbering stage coach with its complement of four or six mules. There was ever to be feared an attack by those devils of the desert, the Cheyennes, Comanches, and Kiowas. Along its whole route the remains of men, animals, and the wrecks of camps and wagons, told a story of suffering, robbery, and outrage more impressive than any language. Now the tourist or business man makes the journey in palace cars, and there is nothing to remind him of Border days; on every hand are the evidences of a powerful and advanced civilization.[8]

6

HAZARDS FACED ON THE TRAIL

The merchants who traveled the Santa Fe Trail had no illusions. They knew that the trip was hazardous. Not all those who set out from Independence would live to see Santa Fe. The travelers would take what precautions they could. The odds were greater that they would survive than that they would not.

Travelers Cope with Illness and Accidents

It is estimated that one out of every twenty pioneers who headed down America's trails to the west died on the way.

More people on the trail died from disease than from any other cause. Malaria, pneumonia, smallpox, measles, and dysentery took their toll. Cholera was the number one killer. Cholera is a bacterial disease that causes severe dehydrating diarrhea, followed by death. People contract cholera from contaminated food and impure water. Wagon trains needed to dispose of human waste in a safe manner. If this was not done, cholera spread to the uninfected. Cholera often spread from one wagon train to another.

Accidents also took their toll. Although wagons moved slowly, people were sometimes crushed beneath the wheels. Drownings were common at river crossings. Accidental shootings were frequent, because many travelers were unfamiliar with the use of firearms.

Weather Extremes Can Bring Disaster

Travel on the Santa Fe Trail brought with it a number of natural challenges. Weather was the most important factor when planning a trip. Sudden winter storms caused the most loss of life to both humans and animals. The prairie was known for the bad snowstorms that it gets in October and April, times when travelers thought snow and ice would not be that much of a problem. Other hazards included hail, high winds, tornadoes, and ice. Hailstones larger than hen's eggs and gale force winds tore the freight wagons' heavy canvas coverings. It required the skills of a sailmaker to repair them.

Most caravans did not travel in winter, when the sub-zero cold came across the plains directly from the frozen Arctic wastes. Spring was the favorite time for travel, because the weather was mild and prairie grass was plentiful. The growth of the grass was very important to the timing of the trains leaving Missouri. If they left too early, they risked getting out onto the prairie before there was enough grass available for their livestock. Summers were harsh. The midday heat often reached the hundred-degree mark as the caravan crossed Kansas. In dry weather, clouds of dust rose from the wagon wheels. Rain turned the dust to clinging mud. There were two main variations in the trail, called wet and dry routes. During dry weather, the trains tended to follow the banks of the nearest river. In wet weather, the trail followed higher ground parallel to the streams.

Violent rainstorms rolled across the prairies. The crashing thunder and flashing lightning often caused the train's livestock to stampede. At most times, mules are willing and patient animals. In a storm, they can act as absurdly as a Texas steer in a stampede. Off they would dash. Usually they stopped when they entangled each other. Sometimes, in their mad rush, they

The Santa Fe Trail passed through dry regions such as the Canadian River valley in New Mexico.

SOURCE DOCUMENT

WE NOW ENCOUNTERED A GREAT DEAL OF WET WEATHER; IN FACT THIS REGION IS FAMOUS FOR COLD PROTRACTED RAINS OF TWO OR THREE DAYS' DURATION. STORMS OF HAILSTONES LARGER THAN HEN'S EGGS ARE NOT UNCOMMON, FREQUENTLY ACCOMPANIED BY THE MOST TREMENDOUS HURRICANES. THE VIOLENCE OF THE WIND IS SOMETIMES SO GREAT THAT, AS I HAVE HEARD, TWO ROAD-WAGONS WERE ONCE CAPSIZED BY ONE OF THESE TERRIBLE THUNDER-GUSTS; THE RAIN, AT THE SAME TIME, FLOATING THE PLAIN TO THE DEPTH OF SEVERAL INCHES. IN SHORT, I DOUBT IF THERE IS ANY KNOWN REGION OUT OF THE TROPICS, THAT CAN "HEAD" [LEAD] THE GREAT PRAIRIES IN "GETTING UP" [PREPARING FOR] THUNDER-STORMS, COMBINING SO MANY OF THE ELEMENTS OF THE AWFUL AND SUBLIME.[1]

Trader Josiah Gregg related his memories of a storm on the Santa Fe Trail.

crushed their drivers to death. After the rain, trains kept a careful lookout for flash floods. Dry creek beds could turn into raging torrents in a matter of minutes.

Wildfires Sweep Across the Prairies

Prolonged heat or drought turned the prairie grasses into straw. Night guards kept an eye out for prairie fires. Lightning was the cause of most prairie fires. The Plains peoples sometimes set fires to drive game to the edge of creeks, where they were easily hunted. Writer Matt Field reported in the *New Orleans Picayune* in 1839.

The whole camp was disturbed at the changing of the guard, and our eyes were opened upon a scene of wild splendor that at once enchained us in boundless admiration. The fire had approached to us within four or five hundred yards, and we could hear the tall grass crackling in the flames and the dull roar of the night wind like an angry spirit. . . . The trees and brush that lined the creek added to the enchantment of the scene. As the fire swept on, the light seen through the trees appeared in all kinds of fantastic and curious shapes . . . The flames (now racing steadily forward, and again darting furiously in side-long and eccentric directions . . .) formed for a lively imagination things of fantasy.[2]

Insects Provide Constant Annoyance

Caravans traveled in the center of a cloud of insects. The insects hovered over wagons that had thin sheets of buffalo meat drying in the prairie sun. Blowflies laid their eggs on the meat. Teamsters often consumed harmless blowfly larva with their jerky. In the waist-high prairie grasses lived horseflies, several times larger than their eastern cousins. When dozens of them settled on a team of mules, the animals often jumped into a full run. If the winds were not brisk enough to blow the flies away, the train was forced to travel at night to avoid the heat.

Travelers were set upon by gnats, chiggers, and lice. Mosquitoes were everywhere on the trail. Susan Magoffin wrote in 1846, "I drew my feet up under me, wrapped my shawl over my head, till I almost smothered with heat, and listened to the din without. . . . Millions upon millions were swarming around me—their knocking against the carriage reminded me of a hard rain."[3]

Indian Attacks Are a Rarity

Indian attacks were not a major danger on the Santa Fe Trail. In fact, the risk of death from this cause probably was about the same for the emigrants as for the people who stayed at home on the western frontier. A more common event was the running off of stock and theft from the wagons.

There were wide differences between the tribes along the Santa Fe Trail. The easternmost parts of the trail ran through the homeland of the Osage and Kansa Indians. The word on the trail was that members of these tribes would steal anything they could lay hands on, but they were seldom life-threatening. Other tribes included Kiowas, Arapahoes, and Plains Apaches. Farther west, early travelers on the Santa Fe Trail faced attack from the Pawnee. Bands often swept down from behind Pawnee Rock to attack smaller parties. Contact with the whites had brought them smallpox. Soon their numbers were greatly reduced.

The Cheyenne and Sioux sometimes followed the buffalo as far south as the trail, but were seldom violent. It was the Comanche, about twenty thousand strong in the early days of the trail, who were most likely to attack. Yet, despite the many encounters between whites and American Indians, only eight

Pawnee Rock in Kansas was a familiar landmark on the Santa Fe Trail.

traders were killed along the trail by native peoples during the first decade after Becknell's journey.

River Crossings Are Dangerous

Crossing rivers and creeks caused casualties. Sometimes a heavily laden mule would lose its footing on the river bottom, or sink into quicksand and drown. The heavy wagons often became stuck in the mud at river crossings. Originally, their freight capacity was about three thousand pounds. Later wagons could carry nearly double that. Wagons that were watertight when they left Missouri might open a seam en route. Caravans often came to a river at flood stage. Usually they would not endanger their cargo. They waited until the water subsided before attempting to wade across.

No two trips found the trail in identical condition. It took all the skills of the wagon boss to direct his caravan in safely crossing a raging stream or a marshy slough—a place of deep mud. Even smaller creeks

River crossings on the Santa Fe Trail brought many hazards to the freight caravans.

presented problems. Flash floods often dug deep gullies too wide to cross easily. The teamsters had to dig out a graded approach on both sides of the gully, to form what was called a cut-down. The wagons would tilt perilously down. The steep climb out often required the full strength of men and animals.

Equipment Breakdown Creates Problems

Most wagon trains made every effort to see that their equipment was in top shape before heading west. Between Council Grove and Santa Fe, only Bent's Fort offered repair facilities, and then only for a few years. There were no repair facilities on the southern route. Once past Council Grove, the traders were on their own. Some traders cached, or buried, their supplies until they could return with needed livestock or wagon. Most traders carried spare wagon parts with them. Any train that took the route to Bent's Fort later had to cross Raton Pass. Most trains chose to avoid this added hazard, so members of the caravan had to do the work of blacksmiths, carpenters, wheelwrights, and gunsmiths.

The wagons themselves were sturdily built. Still, the hundreds of miles of jolting, soaking, and baking took an inevitable toll. Along most of the trail, few trees grew. If an axle broke, there was no timber to fashion into a replacement. As the sun parched the wood in the massive wheels, they contracted. It became necessary to reduce the iron bands encasing them. The amateur blacksmiths then reattached them to the wheel with rawhide.

Customs Officials Are a Final Hazard

Not all the hazards of the trip came from nature and American Indians. The greed of Santa Fe officials threatened to restrict the trip's profitability. When the trains neared Santa Fe, merchants often hurried ahead of their wagons. They wanted to clear customs first. The first merchants to place goods on sale got the highest prices. In Santa Fe, the merchants employed local clerks. The clerks translated the train's cargo manifests into Spanish. Then the merchants hurried to the Palace of the Governor to pay the duty.

Duty was levied on the value listed on each wagon's invoice. Originally, the duty set by law was 100 percent. After haggling, the governor might agree to collect 35 percent.[4] Later, the governor changed the system. He would assess a flat sum on each wagon, five hundred dollars to $950. He seemed to set the amount at whim.

The traders found ways to combat the high tariff. Sometimes, they stopped within a day's journey of Santa Fe and transferred the goods from three wagons into one. They then burned the two empty wagons. They hitched the mules to the heavy-laden one. On entering Santa Fe, they paid only one wagon's duty. The officials also tried to collect a tax for exporting gold and silver when the merchants headed home.

Some of the wagons came with hollow axletrees, in which the precious cargo could be hidden.

Rewards Outstrip Hazards

Those traveling the Santa Fe Trail usually thought the rewards outstripped the hazards. Historian Walter Prescott Webb summed up their feelings. He called the trip west "high adventure." Overcoming the hazards on the Santa Fe Trail, he thought, was as exciting as the adventures of the Spanish conquistadors or today's astronauts.

★ A MEETING WITH COMANCHEROS ★

The American traders on the Santa Fe Trail were not the first European Americans to roam the plains. For two hundred years, Spanish hunters, called Cibolers, had killed buffalo on the prairies. The buffalo meat was an important source of food for the settlements in New Mexico. From Santa Fe, merchants also exported dried buffalo meat to northern Mexico. The Cibolers were numerous enough to disturb the Cheyenne. The Cheyenne and Cibolers fought pitched battles over hunting rights. The Cibolers then shifted their area of activity. They hunted in the Comanche territory of the high plains.

Some of the small merchants of Santa Fe followed the Cibolers into Comanche territory. Because they traded with the Comanche, they were called Comancheros. New Mexico signed a formal peace with the Comanche in 1786. By then, the Comanche had driven the Apache from the plains. In the treaty, the Comanche promised to drive out any non-Spanish intruders. As a result, the

Comanche hunted buffalo on the prairie regions crossed by the Santa Fe Trail.

Comanche pillaged, killed, and kidnapped in Texas for decades.

By the mid-1800s, the Comancheros slowly changed their role. They ceased being peaceful traders of merchandise. More often, their trade with the Comanche involved whiskey and guns.

Sometimes the American caravans heading for Santa Fe encountered a group of Comancheros. In his 1844 book, *Commerce on the Prairies*, Josiah Gregg tells of one such encounter:

> A few days afterwards we were overtaken by a party of *Comancheros* or Mexican Comanche traders. . . . They had taken to overtake us so as to obtain our protection against the [Comanche]. . . . After selling their animals to the Mexicans, [the Comanche] very frequently take forcible possession of them again, before the purchasers have been able to reach home. These parties of *Comancheros* are usually composed of the indigent and rude classes of the frontier villages. . . . , [They]

collect together several times a year and launch upon the plains with a few trinkets and trumperies of all kinds, and perhaps a bag of bread and another of *pinole*. . . . They barter [them] away to the [Comanche] for horses and mules. The entire stock of an individual trader very seldom exceeds the value of twenty dollars. . . . , [With this] he is content to wander around for several months. . . . [He is] glad to return home with a mule or two as the proceeds of his traffic.

These Mexican traders had much to tell us about the Comanches. . . . [They said] that they were four or five thousand in number. . . . They had perhaps a thousand warriors. . . . The fiery young men had determined to follow and attack us. . . . The chiefs and sages had deterred them by stating that our cannons could kill to the distance of twenty miles. . . . [They could] shoot through hills and rocks and destroy everything that happened to be within their range. The main object of our visitors, however, seemed to be to raise themselves in importance by exaggerating the perils we had escaped from.[5]

Contacts between American freight caravans and groups of Comancheros were usually peaceful. The Comancheros were not strong enough to launch an attack.

For more than half a century, commerce plied the Santa Fe Trail. Many historic events occurred in North America during those years. Each changed the trail in its own way.

The Trail Becomes a Two-Way Highway

7

THE TRAIL IN LATER YEARS

The leading families of Santa Fe soon began outfitting their own trade caravans. The Oteros, Chavezes, Armíjos, and Pereas sent wagons eastward. They carried blankets, raw wool, and buffalo robes. In 1867, Santa Fe trader Don José Perea sent ten wagons up the trail to Kansas City. He recruited his drivers from the village of Placitas. Local men lined up in the plaza. Perea made his choices. Family members left behind knew the trip was dangerous. Some drivers would not return. Mothers and wives locked the image of their family saint in a chest during the man's absence. When their man returned, the saint was taken out. Family members honored it with singing and dancing. If word came of a loved one's death, the family took the saint outside and buried it.

Perea's wagons joined a caravan assembling at Las

Vegas. The caravan included almost four hundred wagons. Some days the wagons traveled eighteen hours a day without stopping. The drivers got only one full meal a day. Twice a day they snacked on a tortilla and an onion. The drivers arrived in Kansas City thin and ragged. They loaded kettles, china, cutlery, furniture, and cloth for the return trip. At night they might marvel at a parade advertising a minstrel show. The drivers had no money to spend on entertainment. They would be paid when they returned home. A driver would receive eight dollars for his several months of work.[1]

Bent's Fort Provides a Santa Fe Trail Way Station

In 1833, the company of Charles and William Bent and Ceran St. Vrain erected a trading post. They selected a spot on the Arkansas River near present-day La Junta, Colorado. During the 1840s, the sturdy adobe and log structure was like a department store for the Santa Fe Trail. It lay at the intersection of several trading routes. The area of the fort was home to thousands of Southern Cheyenne, Arapahos, Kiowa, and other tribes. The company traded sugar, cloth, knives, and general supplies to white mountain men and American Indians. In return, the company received hides and furs.

For caravans, the fort provided a rest stop, repair shop, and resupply station. The fort also provided defense, lodging, and offices. Bent's Fort was built

Bent's Fort offered a restocking point for travelers on the northern route of the Santa Fe Trail.

about a central courtyard. The outer walls contained most of the fort's rooms. William Bent had an office and a bedroom. Business took place in trade and council rooms. A warehouse housed furs and trade goods. The dining room was the largest in the fort. The fort's cook, Charlotte Green, and her husband lived in a room just off the kitchen. Other rooms included a blacksmith's and a carpenter's shop, and a billiard room. There were also quarters for laborers and trappers.

Charles Bent was murdered in Taos in 1847. St. Vrain failed to sell the fort to the Army that year. William Bent abandoned the fort during a cholera epidemic two years later.

The Santa Fe Trail Witnesses an Uprising and an Invasion

American merchants believed that Santa Fe traders were exempt from the high duties levied by Governor Manuel Armíjo. In 1835, Mexico City sent a new governor, Colonel Albino Pérez. In August 1837, all of New Mexico rose in revolt. A mob captured Pérez outside Santa Fe and decapitated him. The following month, Armíjo led his own revolt. He entered Santa Fe without resistance. Mexico City confirmed him as governor. Two hundred dragoons, European-trained soldiers on horseback, arrived to help him keep order.

In 1841, word swept up and down the Santa Fe Trail. The young Republic of Texas' second president, Mirabeau Lamar, was sending an army westward.

Texas claimed that its western boundary was the Rio Grande. That would place both Santa Fe and Taos under Texas control. The New Mexicans considered the Texans to be

The expedition sent by Governor Mirabeau Lamar of Texas failed in its invasion of New Mexico.

godless invaders. The Mexicans thought they were bent on arson, pillage, and murder. In September 1841, they formed an army under Governor Armíjo.

The Texans numbered only three hundred. Austin was only seven hundred miles from Santa Fe. Nevertheless, the Texans roamed for thirteen hundred miles. In summer, the Plains were waterless. Kiowa and Comanche war parties harassed them. When they neared the New Mexico border, the Texans were close to starvation, so they sent an advance party to secure New Mexico's surrender. Instead, Armíjo took them prisoner. If the others surrendered, Armíjo promised, he would send them all home safely. Instead, Armíjo rounded up the Texans. He sent them on foot to imprisonment in Mexico City two thousand miles away. Diplomats from the United States and England helped to gain the release of the survivors.

Thousands of Forty-Niners Use the Southern Route

Gold was discovered in California at Sutter's Mill in 1848. The event set off a great migration westward. The western trails were ten thousand miles shorter than the trip by sea around Cape Horn. Passage by ship cost at least three hundred dollars. Midwestern farmers already had much of what they needed for the overland trip. They possessed teams of oxen and sturdy wagons. They could provision their wagons with food they had grown themselves. For passengers, there was one stage a month between Independence and Santa Fe.

In 1849, most gold-seekers chose the northern route. They followed the Platte River, then crossed the Rockies through South Pass. They descended the Humboldt River and crossed the Sierra Nevada Mountains into California. Other thousands of Forty-Niners chose a southern route. It followed the old traders' route to Santa Fe. These caravans were escorted by U.S. troops. The U.S. Army maintained a Santa Fe garrison of 280 soldiers. Others came to Santa Fe from Fort Smith, Arkansas. From Santa Fe, most followed the Old Spanish Trail, over the Wasatch Mountains and down the Virgin River. The Forty-Niners crossed the Sierras via the Tehachapi and Tejon Passes into California. Others went south. They followed the barren hills along the Gila River. Then they crossed a ninety-mile desert. Their last barrier before the Pacific was the coastal range of the Sierras.

★ SANTA FE IN THE MEXICAN WAR ★

The United States and Mexico disputed the southern boundary of Texas. The armies of the two nations clashed in south Texas in April 1846. The United States declared war the following month. President James Polk ordered General Stephen Watts Kearny to invade the northern provinces of Mexico. On June 26, Kearny headed west from Fort Leavenworth, Kansas. His Army of the West was not large. It consisted of 1,458 soldiers. His artillery consisted of twelve six-pound cannons and four twelve-pound howitzers. The army moved with 1,556 wagons,

3,658 draft mules, and 459 horses.[2] One month and 537 miles later, the army arrived at Bent's Fort.

The Army of the West left Bent's Fort on August 2. Five days later, the Army crossed Raton Pass. In Santa Fe, the people calmly awaited the arrival of the Americans. They had little reason to be loyal to Mexico. Some felt that Mexico had provided them with little more than high taxes and corrupt governors. Others followed the leadership of Governor Manuel Armíjo. Publicly, the governor issued proclamations urging resistance. Privately Armíjo feared what would happen if he fought the Americans. He also worried about what might happen if he did not.

General Kearny sent two agents to Santa Fe. Captain Philip Cooke and a trader named James Magoffin carried a letter from Kearny to Governor Armíjo. It promised Armíjo that those who yielded without fighting would be protected. Magoffin knew Spanish. He was an acquaintance of the governor. The agents, escorted by twelve mounted soldiers, rode into Santa Fe under a flag of truce on August 12. Cooke went to confer with Armíjo. Magoffin sought out his friend, Santa Fe trader Henry Connelley. Connelley assured Magoffin that Armíjo was not committed to resistance.

That night, Magoffin and Cooke dined with the governor. Magoffin translated Kearny's letter for Armíjo. It presented the American claim. The Rio Grande formed the U.S. border with Mexico from source to mouth. It advised the governor to surrender peaceably. No one knows for sure what was agreed upon. A large sum may have changed hands. Magoffin later asked the U.S. government for fifty thousand dollars. He said it was to reimburse him for "secret services rendered during the war."[3]

On August 16, Armíjo led his poorly equipped army out of Santa Fe. Three thousand men took up positions in the narrow pass of Apache Canyon. Kearny's forces approached the next day. Armíjo ordered a sudden withdrawal. Back in Santa Fe, Armíjo loaded money and supplies on pack animals. He fled south, and took all the dragoons with him as bodyguards.

A day later, Kearny's army was in Santa Fe. They had taken the city without firing a shot. On August 19, the formal surrender of New Mexico took place in the Santa Fe plaza. Leading citizens shouted, *"Viva el General."* (Long live the general!) They pressed forward to swear allegiance to the United States. The Santa Fe Trail was again open for American traders.

The Civil War Spreads to New Mexico

Only briefly during the Civil War (1861–65) did the Santa Fe Trail become a battleground. In 1861, three thousand Confederate troops entered New Mexico from El Paso, Texas. General H. H. Sibley led the army, mainly made up of Texans. They hoped to take Fort Union. It would become a base for the conquest of California. Only a thousand regular Union troops opposed Sibley. Supporting them were two regiments of New Mexico volunteers, and two companies of Colorado troops. The Confederate forces easily captured both Albuquerque and Santa Fe.

In March 1862, Union reinforcements arrived from Colorado. As the Confederates advanced through Apache Canyon, they were attacked by Union cavalry, artillery, and infantry. The Southerners retreated in disorder and sought shelter among the rocks along the canyon. That night, Major John Chivington led six companies of Union troops over the mountain and behind Southern lines. They captured and burned the Southern supply train. Helpless without their supplies, the Southern forces withdrew back to Texas, never to return.

Contractors Provide Freight and Passenger Service

During the Civil War, freight wagons rolled west regularly along the Santa Fe Trail. Alexander Majors had the contract to bring supplies to Fort Union. From there, supplies were distributed to posts throughout the west. Majors's firm operated over 3,500 wagons. It employed five thousand men, and owned forty thousand oxen. Majors required his employees to take this pledge: "While in the employ of Alexander [Majors], I agree not to use profane language, not to get drunk, not to treat animals cruelly, and not to do anything else that is incompatible with the character of a gentleman."[4]

Mail came down the Santa Fe Trail by stagecoach. Beginning in 1858, Hockaday and Hall coaches left Independence for Santa Fe on the first and fifteenth of each month. The bruising trip lasted two weeks or more. Passengers who paid 150 dollars one way slept on the coach. They ate hurried meals when the stage stopped to change horses. They gulped down fried pork, boiled beans, and searing coffee.

A Toll Road Conquers Raton Pass

After the Civil War, the possibility of a Comanche attack made travel on the Cimarron cutoff hazardous. Most caravans took the northern route through Raton Pass. Richard Wooton, known to thousands as Uncle Dick, was one of the legends of the Santa Fe Trail. Since 1836, he had been a trapper and caravan master. Wooton decided something could be done about the Raton Pass obstructions. In the late 1850s, he obtained charters from the legislatures of Colorado and New Mexico. Then he began building a toll road.

His work crews blasted away Devil's Rock, the biggest obstruction. They straightened the kinks. On

From his homestead in Raton Pass, New Mexico, Uncle Dick Wooton operated a toll road.

his road, a mule team could make the turns without bending sharply in the middle. The toll road stretched twenty-seven tortuous miles over the eight-thousand-foot pass. Wooton charged $1.50 for each heavy wagon or stagecoach. Riders paid twenty-five cents. He charged five cents each for livestock. American Indians crossed for free. He kept the silver coins he received in an empty whiskey barrel. When it was full, he carried it to a bank in nearby Trinidad. The venture paid off handsomely. In one fifteen-month period, the road took in almost ten thousand dollars.

The Railroads End Use of the Santa Fe Trail

The toll road prospered only briefly. Then the railroads put it out of business. The railroads closed the Santa Fe Trail one section at a time. In 1863, the Kansas Pacific Railroad pushed west from Wyandotte, Kansas, across from Kansas City. Three years later the Atchison, Topeka, and Santa Fe (ATSF) began building westward from Topeka. By 1872, the ATSF had reached the bend of the Arkansas River. At the point where Becknell first crossed the river, Dodge City arose.

The ATSF pushed west to Pueblo, Colorado, where it turned toward Santa Fe and California. There was one major problem: control of the Raton Pass. The Rio Grande Railroad also claimed the right of way there. Men armed with rifles and shovels faced each other. The Rio Grande Railroad backed down. The first train chugged over the pass in December 1878. The Raton Tunnel opened in September 1879. The

The coming of the railroad brought an end to the commerce of the Santa Fe Trail.

main line of Santa Fe Railroad bypassed the city of Santa Fe. The railroad said it lay too high in the hills. The following year, a seventeen-mile spur was built to the city from Lamy, New Mexico, on the main line. The first train chugged into Santa Fe on February 9, 1880. The days of using the Santa Fe Trail to haul freight were over. It would still be used by immigrant settlers and local travelers.

★ FOLLOWING THE SANTA FE TRAIL TODAY ★

There is no one best way to follow the Santa Fe Trail today. It does not matter at which end you start. The Santa Fe Trail is a two-way road today, as it was over a century ago. You can begin at Santa Fe's historic Plaza. You can start at tiny New Franklin, Missouri, or you can start and finish anywhere in between. Only the sturdiest will attempt to walk the route, emulating those mule drovers who walked beside their freight wagons.

You will have a choice of transportation. Most of the trail is easily accessible by road. Driving makes it easy to forget the short distances the caravans traveled each day. The journey from downtown Independence, Missouri, to Red Bridge Park takes less than half an hour by car. On the trail, it was the first midday "nooning" rest spot, a half-day's travel. You might choose the slower pace of bicycles. This is recommended only for experienced riders in good physical condition. On the western sections of the trail, many of the grades are steep. Climbing them requires low gears. Altitudes rise to well over a mile above sea level. The strenuous exercise taxes even the healthiest lungs. Rarely, organized groups of horsemen travel the entire distance in the saddle. The trip can last almost two grueling months.

To follow the route of the traders, it is a good idea to use a specialized guidebook. One of the best is *Following the Santa Fe Trail: A Guide for Modern Travelers*, by Marc Simmons. Skilled docents (well-trained guides) staff the many historic sites along the route. They are invaluable sources of information. Those contemplating a trail adventure might wish to join The Santa Fe Trail Association. Its twelve chapters cover the trail from Santa Fe to Independence. Student membership is only ten dollars a year. Its members are active in marking the trail, restoring historic sites, and conducting programs on trail history. It can be reached at The Santa Fe Trail Association, Santa Fe Trail Center, RR3, Larned, KS 67550, (316) 285-6911 or (316) 285-2054. The Santa Fe Trail Association is online at http://www.santafetrail.org.

8

THE SANTA FE TRAIL TODAY

Many Americans sense the romance of the Santa Fe Trail. They are drawn to visit the actual places that dotted its route. Fortunately, most are easily accessible.

Starting Where the Trail Once Started

A favorite place to start is the tiny settlement of Franklin, Missouri. Today, the population of Franklin is about 181. Approximately eleven hundred people live in nearby New Franklin. A plain granite marker sits squarely in the middle of placid New Franklin's main street. Its chiseled inscription reads: *"Franklin, 'Cradle of the Santa Fe Trail.' This trail, one of the great highways of the world, stretched nearly one thousand miles from Franklin, Missouri to Santa Fe, New Mexico. 'From Civilization to Sundown.'"*

The trail's actual birthplace was several miles south of New Franklin. By 1828, the Big Muddy, as the Missouri River was known, had chased the Franklin residents to higher ground.

Old-timers remember hearing that the pioneers first marked the trail by bending down branches of saplings. They say you can still see the oldest trees, with limbs bent toward the ground at a right angle.

Independence Offers Memories of Trail Driving Days

When Becknell blazed the Santa Fe Trail, Independence, Missouri, was still an Osage gathering place. Six years later, Independence was the seat of brand-new Jackson County. Quickly it became the major outfitting post for Santa Fe Trail merchants. In the 1840s in springtime, ten thousand oxen would be grazing in the town's fields.

Several sites help visitors rediscover this era. Primary among these sites is the National Frontier Trails Center. The museum is housed in a former flour mill. Its displays include covered wagons, pioneer implements, and a look at life on the Santa Fe Trail. The museum, at 318 West Pacific Avenue, is open weekdays from 9 A.M. to 4:30 P.M. from April to October. From November to March, the weekday hours are from 10 A.M. to 4 P.M. Weekend hours are from 12:30 to 4 P.M. The trip west is told in the words of the travelers in the museum's exhibit hall. The museum displays authentic covered wagons, pioneer implements, beautiful murals, and drawings by pioneers. The attached research library is the largest in the country focused on the overland trails. Other Independence sites include the 1859 jail and marshal's home and the 1827 log courthouse.

Larned, Kansas, Presents Two Santa Fe Trail Sites

The Santa Fe Trail Center is a nonprofit regional museum. The center is located two miles west of Larned, Kansas, on Highway K-156. It contains both a museum and a library. The east gallery of the museum goes back to the days before the recorded history of the trail. It evokes a time when millions of buffalo covered the plains.

On display are giant commercial freight wagons, once pulled by oxen and mules across the nearby

The Santa Fe Trail Center in Larned, Kansas, offers visitors a chance to learn about the history and importance of this national landmark.

prairie. The museum is a meeting place for American Indian, Hispanic, and Anglo cultures. It points out that, unlike the other great western trails, the Santa Fe Trail was a two-way link between two different countries and several different cultures. By the early 1840s, the majority of caravans on the trail were owned and operated by New Mexicans. The museum is open daily, 9:00 A.M. to 5:00 P.M., and it is closed Mondays from Labor Day through Memorial Day.

Nearby is Fort Larned National Historic Site, operated by the National Park Service. It preserves a quadrangle of nine restored sandstone buildings. The visitor center features exhibits relating to the Santa Fe Trail.

Dodge City Marks a Turning Point

Dodge City was the point of decision on the Santa Fe Trail. Should the caravan go the mountain route via Bent's Fort and Raton Pass? An unseasonable snowstorm could bring disaster. The grueling longer mountain route added weeks to the trip, but heading south across the Cimarron cutoff meant enduring waterless sandhills and searing heat.

The trail was over forty years old when Fort Dodge was established on the north bank of the Arkansas River in 1865. Seven years later, Dodge City was founded five miles farther west. It quickly became a trade center for the Santa Fe Trail and for buffalo hunters. The railroad reached Dodge City in 1872. Three years later, longhorn cattle flooded into Dodge

Sand dunes in western Kansas provided a challenge for a wagon train's people and animals.

City. They had come hundreds of miles up the trails from Texas. The roaring frontier town's lawmen included Wyatt Earp and Bat Masterson. Visitors today can recapture the flavor of this trail town by visiting Boot Hill Cemetery, the Front Street businesses, and the stone buildings of Fort Dodge.

Revisit a Supply Point at Bent's Fort

Bent's Old Fort National Historic Site is operated by the National Park Service. The park lies along the Arkansas River in southeastern Colorado. It is located on Colorado Highway 194, seven miles east of La Junta and thirteen miles west of Las Animas. The reconstructed fort lies at the end of a quarter-mile path that follows the original Santa Fe Trail. It is open between Memorial Day and Labor Day, 8:00 A.M. to 5:30 P.M. Winter hours are from 9:00 A.M. to 4:00 P.M. During the summer, there is a twenty-minute film, *Castle on the Plains,* shown hourly.

Also during the summer, demonstrators dressed in period costume offer daily living history presentations. Rangers conduct guided tours. A blacksmith operates a forge. He uses the tools and techniques in practice during the years the fort was open. School groups and others can arrange educational tours and demonstrations. There is a fully stocked bookstore and Indian trade room.

Oklahoma Remembers Its Portion of the Trail

The Cimarron Heritage Center was established in 1994 to preserve the history of the Oklahoma portion of the Santa Fe Trail. The museum is located at 1300 North Cimarron (Highway 287 North) in Boise City. It is open 10:00 A.M. to 3:30 P.M., Monday through Thursday; 1:00 P.M. to 4:00 P.M., Fridays and Saturdays; and closed Sundays. The Santa Fe Trail exhibit is the first a visitor encounters upon entering. Photographs and artifacts trace the trail through Cimarron County in the Oklahoma Panhandle.

Nearby is Autograph Rock, a two-hundred-yard-long rock cliff. On it are inscribed hundreds of carved signatures of Santa Fe travelers. They date back as early as 1826. One easily readable name is F. B. Delgado, a noted Santa Fe freighter. Some famous names known to Santa Fe scholars have been worn away by the weather and are barely recognizable. The Rock is located on posted private property and is not accessible to the public without permission.

Fort Union Protects the Santa Fe Trail

Fort Union was built in 1851, during the middle years of the Santa Fe Trail. During its forty-year history, three different forts were constructed. The third Fort Union was the largest in the Southwest. It served as a military garrison, territorial arsenal, and military supply depot. Today the National Park Service operates the Fort Union National Monument at the site. A visitor center has exhibits telling of the fort's construction and of the military units that utilized Fort Union.

Fort Union is located on New Mexico Highway 161, eight miles from exit 366 of Interstate 25 in northeastern New Mexico. It is open from Memorial Day to Labor Day, 8:00 A.M. to 6:00 P.M. In winter it closes an hour earlier. Visitors can use a footpath to tour the ruins of the second fort and the larger third fort. No traces of the first fort remain. Nearby can be seen the largest network of Santa Fe Trail ruts still visible.

Palace of the Governors Remains Intact

Visitors to the Palace of the Governors in Santa Fe have an easy time imagining what the site was like during

Fort Union in New Mexico provided a welcome stop along the Santa Fe Trail.

the years of the Santa Fe Trail. Outside on the sidewalk, about eighty Pueblo people offer their handicrafts daily. Above them is the long porch, called a portal. Prisoners of war were often hung from the portal. The building, first erected in 1610, is today a museum operated by the University of New Mexico. The present building is the result of a major restoration, conducted in 1909 from original plans found in the British museum.

The Palace's spacious ground floor rooms, dominated by portraits of Spanish governors, are dedicated to the various ages of New Mexico history. The Palace, located on the north side of the Plaza, is open seven days a week, from 10:00 A.M. until 5:00 P.M., except from November through March, when it closes on Monday. The large Palace bookshop offers an extensive selection of books on Southwestern topics.

Other Sites

By no means are these the only remaining Santa Fe Trail sites. In several places, you can still see the ruts cut in the soil by passing wagons. The location of these points can be found in guide books, on websites, and at Santa Fe Trail centers.

★ TIMELINE ★

1609—Santa Fe is founded by New Mexico governor Don Pedro de Peralta.

1790—William Becknell is born in Kentucky.

1803—Louisiana Purchase.

1821—Becknell first follows the route that later became known as the Santa Fe Trail.

1822—William Becknell is the first to use wagons to take trade goods over the Santa Fe Trail.

1825—The U.S. government signs a treaty with the Osage people. It gives the United States the right of way for the Santa Fe Trail.
Congress authorizes an official survey of the Santa Fe Trail.

1826—George C. Sibley completes the survey of the Santa Fe Trail.

1827—The town of Independence, Missouri, is founded. By 1832, it is the outfitting point for the Santa Fe Trail.

1832—Independence becomes the starting point for the Santa Fe Trail.

1833—The fur trading post, Bent's Fort, is established on the upper Arkansas River.

1846—Kearny leads his Army of the West to New Mexico over the Santa Fe Trail.

1846 –1848—The Santa Fe Trail is heavily used during the Mexican War.

1849—Westbound gold-seekers and emigrants travel the Santa Fe Trail.

1851—Wagon train owner Francis X. Aubry finds a Santa Fe Trail cutoff that avoids the dry Jornada. It runs from the established route near Cold Spring on the Cimarron River to the Arkansas River.

1860s—The Santa Fe Trail is shortened at its eastern end with the coming of the Santa Fe Railroad.

1866—Wagon trains that previously formed at Council Grove now form at Junction City. The Stage Company moves its outfit from Council Grove to Junction City.

1872—The Santa Fe Railroad is completed to the Colorado border. The use of the Santa Fe Trail as a main transportation route declines sharply.

1880—The railroad reaches Santa Fe in February. The days of the Santa Fe Trail end.

★ CHAPTER NOTES ★

Chapter 1. Becknell Opens the Santa Fe Trail

1. R. L. Duffus, *The Santa Fe Trail* (London: Longmans, Green & Co., 1931), p. 65.

2. William Becknell, "Diary of William Becknell," *Missouri Intelligencer and Boon's Lick Advertiser*, April 22, 1823, p. 2.

3. Ibid.

4. Marc Simmons, *The Old Trail to Santa Fe* (Albuquerque, N. Mex.: University of New Mexico Press, 1996), p. 75.

5. Duffus, p. 68.

6. Ibid., pp. 68–69.

7. The height of mules, donkeys, and horses are measured in hands—with one hand equal to four inches. They are measured from their shoulders.

8. Duffus, p. 81.

9. *"Power: Horse? Mule? Oxen?"* n.d. <http://www.isu.edu/~trinmich/Power.html> (January 5, 2000).

Chapter 2. Background of New Mexico

1. Donald Jackson, ed., *The Journals of Zebulon Montgomery Pike*, Vol. 1 (Norman: University of Oklahoma Press, 1966), p. 384.

Chapter 3. The U.S. and Santa Fe in 1821

1. "Manifest Destiny" was originally defined by *United States Magazine and Democratic Review* editor John L. O'Sullivan in its July–August 1845 edition, and again in the October 13, 1845, issue of the *New York Morning News*.

2. Raymond F. Locke, *The Book of the Navajo* (Los Angeles: Mankind Publishing Company, 1976), pp. 188–189.

3. Ray Allen Billington, *The Far Western Frontier* (New York: Harper & Brothers, 1956), p. 13.

4. Locke, p. 189.

5. James Josiah Webb, *Adventures in the Santa Fe Trade 1844–1847* (Glendale, Calif.: The Arthur H. Clark Company, 1931), pp. 91–93.

Chapter 4. Gathering an Expedition in Independence, Missouri

1. Hobart E. Stocking, *The Road to Santa Fe* (New York: Hastings House, 1971), p. 40.

2. John C. McCoy, quoted in R. L. Duffus, *The Santa Fe Trail* (London: Longmans, Green, & Co., 1931), p. 103.

3. Stocking, p. 34.

Chapter 5. Across Plains, Deserts, and Mountains

1. Henry Inman, *The Old Santa Fe Trail* (Minneapolis, Minn.: Ross & Haines, 1966), pp. 64–65.

2. R. L. Duffus, *The Santa Fe Trail* (London: Longmans, Green, & Co., 1931), p. 144.

3. Stella Drumm, ed., *Down the Santa Fe Trail and Into Mexico, Diary of Susan Shelby Magoffin, 1846–1847* (New Haven, Conn.: Yale University Press, 1962), p. 41.

4. Clyde Porter and Mae Porter, *Matt Field on the Santa Fe Trail* (Norman: University of Oklahoma Press, 1960), p. 137.

5. Josiah Gregg, *Commerce of the Prairies* (Lincoln: University of Nebraska Press, 1967), pp. 50–51.

6. Kenyon Riddle, *Records and Maps of the Old Santa Fe Trail* (Raton, N. Mex.: The Raton Daily Range, 1949), pp. 87–89.

7. Ibid., p. 37.

8. Inman, p. viii.

Chapter 6. Hazards Faced on the Trail

1. Josiah Gregg, *Commerce of the Prairies* (2 vols., New York, 1844), p. 82.

2. Clyde Porter and Mae Porter, *Matt Field on the Santa Fe Trail* (Norman: Oklahoma University Press, 1960), pp. 304–305.

3. Stella Drumm, ed., *Down the Santa Fe Trail and Into Mexico, Diary of Susan Shelby Magoffin, 1846–1847* (New Haven, Conn.: Yale University Press, 1962), p. 34.

4. Porter and Porter, p. 280.

5. Josiah Gregg, *The Commerce of the Prairies* (Lincoln: University of Nebraska Press, 1967), pp. 218–220.

Chapter 7. The Trail in Later Years

1. Marc Simmons, *The Old Trail to Santa Fe* (Albuquerque: University of New Mexico Press, 1996), pp. 171–178.

2. Jack K. Bauer, *The Mexican War* (New York: Macmillan, 1974), p. 130.

3. Paul Horgan, *Great River* (New York: Rinehart & Co., 1954), p. 724.

4. R. L. Duffus, *The Santa Fe Trail* (London: Longmans, Green, & Co., 1931), p. 228.

★ FURTHER READING ★

Alter, Judy. *The Santa Fe Trail.* Danbury, Conn.: Children's Press, 1998.

Blegen, Dan, and Melvin Bacon. *Bent's Fort: Crossroads of Cultures on the Santa Fe Trail.* Brookfield, Conn.: Millbrook Press, 1995.

Drumm, Stella, ed. *Down the Santa Fe Trail and Into Mexico, Diary of Susan Shelby Magoffin, 1846–1847.* New Haven, Conn.: Yale University Press, 1962.

Porter, Clyde, and Mae Porter. *Matt Field on the Santa Fe Trail.* Norman: University of Oklahoma Press, 1960.

Simmons, Marc. *Along the Santa Fe Trail.* Albuquerque: University of New Mexico Press, 1986.

Stocking, Hobart E. *The Road to Santa Fe.* New York: Hastings House, 1971.

Trails West. Washington, D.C.: National Geographic Society, 1979.

Internet Addresses

National Park Service, *Santa Fe National Historic Trail*, October 13, 1998, <http://www.nps.gov/safe/index.htm> (April 19, 2000).

Olsen, Mike, *Santa Fe Trail Net*, June 1999, <http://www.nmhu.edu/research/sftrail/default.htm> (April 19, 2000).

Santa Fe Trail Center Historical Museum Library, *Welcome to the "Heart of the Santa Fe Trail,"* n.d., <http://www.larned.net/trailctr/index.htm> (April 19, 2000).

Santa Fe Trail Association, *The Santa Fe Trail Association Homepage,* n.d., <http://www.santafetrail.org/> (April 19, 2000).

Sween, Nancy, *The Interactive Santa Fe Trail (SFT) Homepage*, 1995–2000,<http://raven.cc.ukans.edu/heritage/research/sft/index.html> (April 19, 2000).

★ INDEX ★